The Longer I Live, the More I Learn

THE LONGER I LIVE, THE MORE I LEARN

a Memoir by
Katherine Harper

Preserving Memories
CHARLOTTE, NC

www.preservememories.net

Published by Preserving Memories, Charlotte, NC.

ISBN 978-0-9742576-9-3   preservingmemories.net

Design: Univoice History, Portland, Mai\ne • univoicehistory.com

Dedication

This book is dedicated to God for giving us
our five wonderful children,
Danny, Jimmy, Margie, Chris and Georgia;
our fourteen grandchildren, and five great grandchildren.
To Ron, my husband of 55 years;
and to the many friends Ron and I have made
around the world over the years.

Acknowledgements

The task of writing this book would not have been successful without the encouragement and help of others.

First, I must acknowledge my own offspring, Dan, Jim, Margie, Chris, and Georgia, for keeping after me to put into writing the story of my life, much like my husband Ron did his. Second, I owe a big thanks to Jack Nelson of Preserving Memories for all the help he gave me in taking what I had to say and editing it into a readable storyline. Next, credit goes to Katie Murphy of Univoice History for the beautiful job she did in designing the book and the dustcover. And not to be forgotten, I must thank Ron for his persistence in wanting to see this project completed and the work he did to bring it about.

Above all else, I feel such humble gratitude to the One who gave me this life, so full of wonderful learning experiences. I thank God for each and every day.

Contents

$\mathcal{P}$reface

"Anyone who stops learning is old, whether at 20 or 80.
Anyone who keeps learning stays young."
—HENRY FORD

$\mathcal{I}$ **can remember learning to dance** as a little girl by standing on my daddy's feet as he would move around the room and then swing me up into the air. I remember learning to count as a five-year-old when sitting on the counter next to the cash register in my daddy's restaurant in downtown Charlotte and Daddy teaching me to make change for the customers paying their bills. From my maternal grandmother I learned I could do anything I set my mind to do. Playing ball with boys from the neighborhood in the middle of Kenilworth Avenue (back when the corner of Kenilworth and East Boulevard was out in the country), I learned I could compete in a boy's world if I learned how to relate.

My whole life has been one of learning. I first contemplated titling this book "Who Am I?" as my continuing search for self-understanding has been a lifelong quest. But then I realized, in many respects I am what I've learned, and that is what I seek to share with others in these pages.

Much of the learning I've done has been hands-on, learning by doing. I learned to love work as a young woman by waiting on tables in my father's restaurant, before moving on to working in Belk's Department Store at age thirteen. Like many mothers, I learned to raise kids by doing it. Likewise, in business, I learned financing by working in several banks, before taking the real learning plunge and starting a business with my husband. Through it all, I have learned we have the ability to do so much more than we think we can do. We just don't know it until we are put in a position where we have to draw on our untapped inner resources.

I was always a questioner, much to the consternation of some of the my school teachers I had. If we don't question, I figured, how will we ever learn? And the day we stop asking "why?" is the day we stop learning. We shut ourselves off from what we don't know when we pretend to have all the answers. I have always been one who is eager to learn more by probing the minds of those who can teach me. Learning is, indeed, always an adventure.

Experience in relating to others has taught me much as well. From my mother I learned there is nothing to be gained from thinking oneself a martyr. Life with Ron has taught me how important it is to know we are loved and how to work together toward common goals. From my children I learned there are always three sides to every story: this person's side, that person's version, and the truth somewhere in the middle.

During times of adversity I have learned how frail we all really are, how brief each individual's life is, and how dependent on divine help we remain. There is much to be learned in the midst of tragedy. After the death of our first child, I was devastated, having hemorrhaged badly and come close to death myself, and then awoke awakening to learn our child was stillborn. A priest came to visit me that evening in the hospital. He pointed out the window at the clear night sky and the brilliant stars up above.

"Now one of those stars belongs to you," he told me. "Don't lose sight of it. Because God gave you an angel in heaven to watch over you, and he'll always be there."

I never forgot that.

I also never forgot how my grandmother used to sit and meditate. She used to call it "practicing the presence of God." I learned to follow her example, and the spiritual foundation I gained from the experience of God's presence gave me courage to speak up when I saw wrongs being committed. My audacity in doing so used to astonish even me. But I came to learn that there may be even more to this side of me, something I get to in what follows.

Through it all I have learned there is a purpose to each person's life and it is important for us to embrace that purpose. The popular contemporary author Anne Rice put it well when she wrote: "There is one purpose to life and one only: To bear witness to and understand as much as possible of the complexity of the world—its beauty, its mysteries, its riddles. The more you understand, the more you look, the greater is your enjoyment of life and your sense of peace. That's all there is to it. If an activity is not grounded in 'to love' or 'to learn,' it does not have value."

What remains for me now is to learn to enjoy retirement and to make the most of it. I certainly find I have more time on my hands, and I think more needs to be done to make use of the wisdom older people have gleaned from their life experiences and to figure out more ways to pass that wisdom on to the next and future generations. Putting my life story together, with the lessons I've learned along the way, is my attempt to make a contribution in that direction.

Milestones in the life of
KATHERINE HODGES HARPER

1933 ..... Born August 23 in Charlotte, NC, to James George and Margaret Hodges.

1951 ..... Graduated from O'Donoghue High School. Met eighteen-year-old Ron Harper on August 3 in Wilmington, NC.

1952 ..... Married Ron Harper on February 12, at St. Patrick's Catholic Church in Charlotte. First baby born in December. Harper offspring now number five children, fourteen grandchildren and five great grandchildren.

1971 ..... Co-founded Ron Harper Associates, Ltd., August 2.

1975 ..... Changed the name of the company to Harper Corporation of America.

1978 ..... Co-founded Harper/Love Adhesives Corporation with husband Ron and N.B. Love of Sydney, Australia.

1980 ..... Co-founded Harper Machinery Corporation.

1986 ..... Campaigned for U.S. Senate in the democratic primary.

1989 ..... Sold Harper Machinery to brother-in-law Dick Harper.

1994 ..... First female conference chair of TAPPI Corrugated Division in its forty-six year history.

1995 ..... First female forum conference chair of Flexographic Technical Association in its forty year history.

1997 ..... Opened Harper Corporation Division in Green Bay, Wisconsin.

2000 ..... Licensed anilox technology to Ruam Zub, Bangkok, Thailand, to form Harper Asia/Pacific; Harper Scientific Division created.

2001 ..... Harper GraphicSolutions™ Division opened.

2002 ..... Celebrated 50th Wedding Anniversary, February 12, at the Renaissance Suites Hotel, Charlotte, N.C.

2003 ..... Licensed Inometa, Herford, Germany, to produce anilox rolls under the name of Harper Graphics (a Harper/Inometa Company).

2003 ..... Central Piedmont Community College, Charlotte, N.C., named the Southwest Campus, the "Harper Campus."

2006 ..... Katherine Harper Teacher's Education Fund established with the Phoenix Challenge Foundation.

2007 ..... Katherine Harper Hall at Appalachian State University named in her honor.

Chapter One

GOD SEES EVERYTHING

I **learned spirituality,** first, from my maternal grandmother. She was from a Hungarian-Gypsy family, with a special knack for spiritual insight. She could see things in the future. When I was a little girl, she predicted my future, saying, "You can't imagine how successful you will be from where you are now."

After she became a widow, living in Charleston, South Carolina, she moved up to New York City and took a job as a housekeeper for a Jewish family. Later, in 1940, when I was about seven years old, she came to live with us. She probably would have come sooner, but she never did like my father, though the two of them finally kind of settled their differences peacefully. I always loved her and we shared the same bedroom.

My friends would come over and Grandma would be so excited to see them. She would go out to the kitchen and bring cookies in for all of us. Everyone would be chatting away.

Grandma would say something and all the others would say to me, "What did she say?"

I'd laugh and say, "I figured you didn't know what she was saying."

Grandma spoke very broken English.

She was also prissy. Even though I slept in the same bedroom with her, I never saw her with her hair uncombed or her face not made up. I never saw her when she was not meticulously dressed. I had to ask, "Grandma, when do you do all this?"

One night I decided to go to bed and pretend I was asleep, positioning the covers so I could sneak and watch her. She sat there and kept looking at the mirror mounted on the side of the dresser, and I would see her glancing my way. It was a wonder she didn't know I was not asleep, because I was afraid to move. She rolled her hair on big metal rollers and she creamed her face, Pond's cream I think it was. I wondered how she could sleep with those heavy metal rollers in her hair.

I woke up early the next morning and watched her again to see how she did her face. She combed her hair and played with her little curls all over her head, and then she put cream on her face again and then makeup. I will always remember the rouge, because she just took a tissue and dabbed it on, nothing on her eyebrows or eyes. Then she got dressed.

She would then walk four blocks up the street and attend the early morning mass at the Catholic church. Grandmother was faithfully religious, though there was a time when she lived in New York when she didn't attend church. She had gone to the confessional at a church in Brooklyn. The priest, unable to understand her broken English, told her not to come back until she could speak good English. He said he couldn't absolve her of anything. So she just quit going.

Fortunately for her, after she came to live with us she found there were beautiful nuns and priests at St. Patrick's in Charlotte. The nuns would let her enter through the convent so she didn't have to climb the steps to the front door of the church. I don't think she ever missed a day until near the end of her life, and she would faithfully attend the novena on Wednesday evenings as well.

She made spirituality so real and so natural. She was always talking about God in a friendly way. She'd sit in her rocking chair near the window in the dining room, where her African violets blossomed on the window sill, and pray. In the morning she'd say her prayers, guided by her little prayer book. Then again, in the afternoon, she'd be in the same place, praying. She said she did it to keep God's presence.

One day I asked her, "What do you mean by 'keeping God's presence'?"

I never forgot her response. She said, "He hears you. He sees you every day. God can see everything."

I couldn't help responding, "Everything? Grandma, you mean, when we go to the bathroom?"

"Yep," she replied, "that is all part of nature. God created it."

"But Grandma, when we take a bath, too; when we are naked?"

And she said, "He isn't seeing anything He didn't create."

"You just remember," she continued, "good or bad, He is there, but He is there to watch over you. He sees everything you do, so you always want to be careful how you behave. But He is a loving father, so He is going to watch you and try to come through and say to you, 'Don't do certain things.' God is with you every moment of every day. He watches over you."

She put into my head the notion that we are all here through the grace of God, and as long as we stay in that grace, nothing is impossible for us. Grandmother never used God to instill fear. She also never talked about the devil, other than telling me, "You don't have to worry about the devil as long as you are doing the right things and pleasing God." Her words made sense to me.

I never forgot those lessons: Not only does God care for us and watch over us, He also communicates with us, tells us what we need to do.

By the time I was in the sixth grade, Grandma's health had begun to fail. She spoke to me about her death, wanting me to be prepared for her passing and telling me how she wanted me to react when she died. She said she wanted me to celebrate when she passed away, because, as she put it, "That is the day I get to see our Father in heaven."

She also told me she didn't want me to wear black. And she told me she had told my mother and my aunt the same. And she wanted me to play the piano on the day she died as much as I could possibly play. Grandma was the one who first got me started on the piano, arranging for me to get my early lessons from one of the sisters at the convent. She was the whole reason I took up playing the piano. Grandma would sit and listen to me practice at home for hours at a time. I don't know how she stood it sometimes. But she would sit there in her rocking chair and attentively listen like I was a concert pianist on a stage. She told me she wanted me to play all day long the day she died.

Of course, when Grandma died in 1944, Mother, my aunt, everyone, they all wore black. The first thing I did in the morning was to start playing the piano, one of the songs Grandma loved. My mother was at my side almost immediately. She reached for the lid to the piano keys and slammed it shut, almost catching my fingers. I started crying and tried to tell her, "But it is what Grandma wanted." My protests went unheeded. For the rest of the day I wasn't able to play the piano and I finally quit my attempts because I knew I would probably end up getting a spanking. I was pretty confused.

When we went to the funeral home, Grandmother looked like she was sleeping peacefully in the casket. They did follow Grandma's wishes and dressed her in a colorful aqua-marine dress, and put a little rouge on her lips and cheeks. Her skin was like silk. Her hair was nicely done. She looked real pretty. I reached up and touched her, and she was ice cold, which scared me more than anything. This wasn't the warm cuddly grandmother I had known and loved. And I remembered how she told me our bodies are only a shell.

The things Grandma taught me have stayed with me down to the present.

Daddy, he always was a dapper fellow. Here he is in 1935.

Chapter Two

MY DADDY THE CHEF

I can still picture him behind the counter preparing meals in the restaurant. My daddy was a good-looking man, very handsome, with thick, dark, wavy hair. He was unmistakably Greek, even if his name, from the time he immigrated to the U.S. in about 1907 at age sixteen, was Jim Hodges.

Daddy prided himself on his good looks, to the point of vanity. He would get his hair styled and his fingers manicured, and he would meticulously groom himself. He dressed impeccably, buying his suits at Tate Brown's, the best men's clothing store in town. Even when working in the restaurant, where he wore the usual button-up "cook shirt" and nice, white pants, with a white apron and chef's hat, he always looked sharp.

Up until I was three years old, he had a little restaurant in uptown Charlotte on South Tryon Street, right across the street from the *Charlotte Observer* and three blocks from the Square, where the city buses would drop off passengers in the old days. Later, for many years, the Arnold Palmer Cadillac dealership occupied the spot where Daddy's restaurant had been. He called his restaurant the Little American Lunch, which was not much more than a counter and a couple of tables, plus the kitchen, with the grill up front.

These days people might call someone like him a cross between a fast order cook and a gourmet chef. Though he had no formal training, he could cook anything. He had taught himself. Occasionally he would look at recipes, but mostly he carried his own recipes with him in his head or made things up on the go. He did all the preparation and cooking, cut his own meat, everything.

The Little American Lunch served breakfast, lunch and dinner to people working in downtown Charlotte. The place offered quick and easy meals for the most part, but Daddy still could be pretty creative at times. He could never just cook pork chops and have them turn out all greasy. Doing something to the pork chops before cooking them to make them extra special was important to him.

Everything he did was an effort to be better than the restaurant around the corner, and there were a lot of little restaurants downtown back then, most of them owned and run by Greeks. But competition never bothered him. He was best friends with all the Greeks in town. He'd say, "People have to have at least two good meals a day." There was always going to be another hungry customer.

Most of what he cooked was all-American cuisine: oatmeal, grits, scrambled eggs and such for breakfast. He was good at planning menus and using everything. If he had roast beef for lunch one day, whatever was left would be beef hash the next day. He made the best hash in the world. Corn beef one day would be corn beef hash the next. Seldom was any food thrown out. He was a magician when it came to his concoctions.

Occasionally he would have a Greek dish. These would take much longer to prepare. In the springtime he liked to fix lamb. To this day I wish I could find somebody who could cook lamb like he did. He would use the fresh spring vegetables, handpicked at the market, and bake the lamb with things like squash. I remember him telling me how important it was to pick the smaller vegetables, whether it was squash, okra, eggplants, or whatever. The smaller ones, he told me, are the more tender and flavorful vegetables.

When cooking he used every spice in the world. He would buy his spices wholesale in the old kind of Mason jars. Nothing was ever labeled. They used to all look the same to me on the shelf, but he would use a little of one, smell what he was cooking; add a little of another, smell it again. He knew what he was doing.

The La Fayette Grill, my daddy's restaurant, in 1953.

There were generally two or three people working for him, white waitresses and African-American dishwashers. Mother also helped out much of the time, seating customers, waiting on tables and taking the money. If they were short on help, Mom was the designated dishwasher.

Daddy liked to use every pot and pan available. I remember helping mother once with the dishwashing when I got older. I had to stand at the sink and wash dishes the whole time. If he melted butter and poured it out, he would need the pot washed before he would do something else. These were heavy, cast-iron restaurant pots and pans. Keeping up with him was a chore.

I recall asking Mother "Why does Daddy use so many pots and pans?"

She just said, "That's him."

He was equally demanding when it came to cleanliness, and absolutely unforgiving if someone didn't clean a mess up immediately. If Daddy's apron got greasy, it was in the laundry and he would have another to put on right away. No one went home at night until everything was cleaned off and wiped down.

But when it came to baking, he wasn't as good as Mother. Daddy couldn't bake desserts. Mother made great cakes, pies, the best banana pudding in the world. He would make the rice pudding, which was always made with the leftover rice from the day before. But she had him beat in the desserts department, and when she started getting rave reviews, he actually made her stop cooking desserts for awhile.

Daddy moved the restaurant business to a new location in 1936, when I was about three years old. Still near the uptown district, on College Street, he called his new place Jim's Grill. The fare was much the same and business just boomed. It was incredible. During World War II, which began in December of 1941, following the Japanese attack on Pearl Harbor, Charlotte was a staging area for the military, and Daddy's restaurant became a favorite among servicemen and local working people alike.

He had a reputation for great hamburgers. There were times during the war when rationing made getting meat difficult. If he couldn't get the beef he wanted, he would take whatever he could get and mix it with pork, which wasn't rationed. The special seasoning he added made his burgers a hit.

Such a hard worker he was. I remember how he was always up and out early before the rest of the family got up in the morning. He would open at 6:00 to catch the before-work crowd and work through the lunch period. After lunch he always came home for a nap, generally around 2:30. Then he'd be back to work at 5:00 to begin preparations for dinner and work up until 9:00 or 10:00. When he got home at the end of the day, he'd pour himself half a glass of liquor, drink it and go to bed.

Jim's Grill did well through the war years. Mother used to worry about him taking all the money he made to the bank, which was two blocks away. He insisted on doing it at night, filling up a brown grocery bag with money on the bottom and stalks of celery and such on the top so it looked like he was carrying groceries. He'd put the money in the deposit slot at the bank. All his hard work was paying off.

Chapter Three

CHILDHOOD IN CHARLOTTE

Born **August 23, 1933,** the year that Franklin Delano Roosevelt first became president, I have spent nearly my entire life living in Charlotte. I began life right smack in the middle of downtown. During my early years Charlotte was a very different place from what it is now, really just a small community. And in many ways it was another era back then. A new home cost an average of $5,759 in 1933, the average income was about $30 a week, and gasoline was a whopping 10¢ a gallon.

Daddy was working as a cook at the Barringer Hotel, but it was soon afterward that he opened the Little American Lunch on South Tryon. We lived across the street on the second floor, up over a merchandise store. My most poignant recollection is of the big billboard sign hanging over the merchandise store advertising Dunlop tires, showing a little boy holding a candle indicating it was time to "re-tire."

We only lived there until I was three years old, so I don't remember much about the place. I do recall my brother George saving the change he found lying around by dropping the coins through a knothole in a floor-board. He must have thought we would always live there and someday he would be rich. Well, when we moved, no one was going to tear up the floorboards for him to retrieve his money, and his savings all got left behind.

I have clearer memories of our next residence, this one on South College Street. We lived on the second floor again, in an apartment over a store that was next door to Daddy's new restaurant (Jim's Grill). The entrance and stairway to our apartment was only about twenty feet from the doorway to the restaurant.

Here I am at about age two, in 1935, along with my brother Alfred.

For a family of five, there wasn't much more room in this apartment than there had been in the last one we lived in. I remember three small bedrooms: One for my folks, one for my two older brothers—George, ten years older, and Alfred, twenty-two months older than me—and the third little bedroom that was mine. There was no central heat and the place could get plenty cold in the wintertime. I would get up in the mornings and feel the chill as soon as my feet touched the linoleum floor. Needless to say it didn't take me long to get to the kitchen where there was a little gas potbelly stove, the one source of heat in the house. I'd have to wait until my brothers had their turn in the kitchen getting dressed, then I would rush in and get myself dressed.

I had my most memorable Christmas in that little apartment when I was six years old. We all went to bed Christmas Eve, wide-eyed and bushy-tailed, and couldn't wait until morning. My brother Alfred and I were up at dawn and we ran to the living room. We got to the door

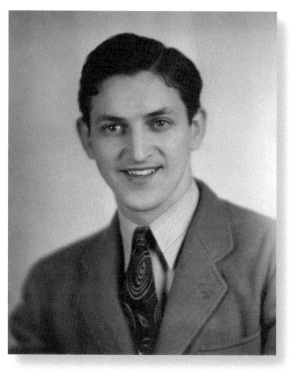

My brother George at the time of his high school graduation in 1941.

and it was locked. Peering in the keyhole, we could see the key sticking in from the other side. We began to knock frantically, which alerted our mother. She wanted to know what was going on. "It's Christmas and Santa locked the door," we cried.

My brother George had slipped into the living room during the night and had locked the door behind him, then fallen asleep on the couch. We finally managed to wake him, without waking up Daddy. George thought it was pretty funny, locking us out when he was in with all the presents. We didn't see anything funny about it, but our distress quickly faded when we walked in and there were all these gifts.

It was incredible. I got everything from a baby doll with a carriage to a play ironing board. My brothers also did well, getting everything they wanted plus more. I just could not believe how wonderful Santa was.

Alfred and I just knew—absolutely—that there was a Santa Claus, because we knew our parents were not rich. Whenever we would ask our

My parents, Jim and Margaret Hodges, 1935.

parents to buy something for us, we could expect the usual reply, "Don't depend on it." Also, Daddy had become angry at us earlier and told us there wasn't going to be a Christmas.

Only later did we learn what had happened. Mother was determined to give her kids a Christmas, and she had secretly taken money out of the cash register at the restaurant when she helped out. She took just a little at a time, so Daddy wouldn't notice the money missing. And she went and put toys on layaway at the local department stores. She wasn't going to let us go without toys. Later she told me, "I didn't care how mad your dad got; you kids were going to have a Christmas."

Now, Daddy didn't know what mother had done, so on Christmas Eve, wanting to make up for what he had said, he went out and bought toys for all of us as well. Mom said they had a big laugh about it when they both came out in the middle of the night with their respective loads of gifts for the children. That is how we got a double Christmas.

Afterward we started hearing, "Don't expect the same thing next year, because Santa Claus got the message wrong." Well, by the time the next year rolled around, I had started having my doubts about Santa Claus. First, there was the night Alfred took the B-B gun he'd received for Christmas and went running into our parents' bedroom, shouting "Daddy, look!" And Daddy sat straight up in bed, and my brother pulled the trigger and shot him right between the eyes.

Daddy went chasing after him, but Mother grabbed Daddy and told him, "It wasn't his fault. I told you not to get him a B-B gun. And you shouldn't have loaded it."

Well, that exchange saved Alfred from getting spanked, but it also gave me my first inkling there wasn't a Santa Claus. Then, a little girl at school told me there was no Santa Claus. I was mad at her for telling me.

———— ⚬₪₪⚬ ————

School for me began when we lived there on South College Street. I attended first and second grade in what was then called the Second Ward, which was a ways from where we lived, down and off College Street. This was in 1939, two years prior to America's entry into World War II. Daddy had a black fellow who worked for him named Leroy, and it was part of Leroy's responsibility to walk us kids to school every morning and meet us when we were ready to come home.

Leroy was strong. Walking to school, Alfred and I would sometimes grab onto his arms, and he would hold us up with his arms outstretched to his sides and carry us down the street.

One day when Leroy was in the kitchen at the restaurant, he leaned over for something and I saw all these marks on top of his head.

I couldn't help but ask, "Leroy, what are all those marks on top of your head?"

He laughed and said, "Those are roadmaps, Honey."

"Roadmaps?" I inquired further.

And he put his head down and pointed to one of the marks and told me it represented such and such a street, and this other one was another street, and so on. I didn't know whether he was telling me the truth or not.

Later Daddy told me, "Child, those are knife marks, left over from fights he has been in. He calls them roadmaps because he can remember where every fight he was in took place."

Poor Leroy. He would get into a fight, get arrested, and his family would call Daddy. Sometimes Daddy went and bailed him out immediately. Other times he let him stay and cool his heels a couple of days. But Daddy always made sure he had cigarettes while he was in jail because he was eager to have Leroy come back to work for him.

Leroy may have been a street fighter, but our father had complete confidence in him. He trusted him more than he did a lot of white folks. Leroy never walked us all the way to school but just took us to a certain spot and let us go the last couple of blocks on our own. Likewise, he would wait for us at that same spot in the afternoons to walk us home.

I finally became curious and asked my mother why Leroy didn't walk us all the way to and from school. I never forgot Mother's response, because it created a new category in my thinking and new reasons to be afraid. She explained how the neighborhood we walked through on our way to school used to be an up-and-coming place to live but had since gotten so bad only "white trash" lived there.

Of course, I couldn't imagine white trash. I knew what trash was, but most trash wasn't white. Well, Mother explained it all to me and afterward I felt scared every time we passed through the "white trash neighborhood." This was still during the Great Depression. Life was awfully tough for some people. People living in that neighborhood were real, real poor back then.

Our playground was the streets of Charlotte, mainly Trade and College. The Trade Street train yards were not far away. Going there was a no-no for us, but in among the empty boxcars was where we often slipped off to play. Most of my playmates in those early days were the "colored" children who lived nearby. We called them "negroes." I played with them all the time, which made racism a confusing notion to me later on when I learned about it.

We learned why the train yards were a forbidden place for us to play the day my brother George closed the door and trapped himself inside one of the empty boxcars. I forget how long he was in there, and he only got out after some railroad employee helping to shunt the boxcars around heard him screaming. The worst for George came later when Daddy got hold of him and thrashed the hell out of him.

I don't recall much about my early schooling in the Second Ward school. But I know by second grade and the beginning of third, I was actively involved in theater and preparing to play a role in a drama called Tom Thumb's Wedding. I just thought my being an actress and being in a real play was the greatest thing in the world.

Unfortunately, my career as an actress was cut short because our family moved again when I was seven years old. Daddy was having great

Here I am again with my brother Alfred, 1937.

success running Jim's Grill. He managed to save up $4,700 and bought a home for us on Kenilworth Avenue, near the intersection with East Boulevard. I'm sure Daddy was eager to display his success, but I had also come down with a severe case of the flu, and a doctor told my mother and father we had to move to the country because life in the crowded streets of Charlotte was not healthy for little children.

Being in our new home on Kenilworth was like living in the country back in those days. The place was like paradise to us, with plenty of open space where we could run out and play and not have to worry about a thing. There was so little traffic we could even play ball in the middle of the street.

Daddy always wanted to have the best and he furnished our new home with some of the best things available. He bought a dining room set. It was Duncan Phyfe, the most expensive furniture at the time. He bought a fancy velvet couch, with carved woodwork along the edges. My maternal grandmother came to live with us soon after we moved into our new home and she was beside herself over the extravagance. She quickly put a sheet over the couch so we could sit on it. Grandmother was always a practical person.

I still feel a certain amount of nostalgia for Charlotte in the old days when I was a young girl growing up. By the late 1930s buses had mostly replaced the old streetcars. There wasn't a lot of traffic, but the old-timers used to complain about it nonetheless. There were even a few traffic lights installed.

They had hitching posts in some areas, left over from former days when people came to town by horse and buggy. We'd still see horses in town sometimes. The iceman delivered big blocks of ice in a horse-drawn ice wagon. People didn't have refrigerators back then and used to purchase ice from the iceman to keep things cool in their iceboxes. I remember old junk collectors coming around as well with horse-drawn wagons, collecting recyclable trash. There was also the slop man, who would come pick up discarded foodstuff to feed hogs on the farms. Daddy used to get fresh hams in the fall in return for letting the slop man empty his slop can.

Downtown was mostly made up of small business establishments and big department stores. On the Square there was Kress and Woolworth's. I used to love the lunch counter at Woolworth's. Belk's Department Store and Efird's were nearby. The Perry Mincey furniture store was on College Street, a place everyone thought was the quality shop in Charlotte. A little further on was the old feed store. I loved that place because they always had little chicks. We got to know the owner well and he would allow us to come in and play with the baby chicks.

It is hard to believe how much has changed. Who would have thought Charlotte would grow to be the metropolis it is today?

My older sister, Alice, 1922.

Chapter Four

FAMILY BACKGROUND

I **didn't know about my sister** until I was fourteen years old. We were living in our home on Kenilworth Avenue. Dad had built a big cabinet out on the back screened porch, with an icebox in it and a bunch of drawers. One day I went back there looking for something and got a bit nosy, seeing all the drawers and wondering what was in them. I started opening and closing drawers. Most of them were full of linens and other things my mother had stored away. Then I opened another one and there were all these photographs of a dead person lying in a coffin.

I ran into the house with the pictures and asked, "Who is this?"

My mother responded in a perturbed voice, "Where did you find that?"

Mother only whipped me once, and that was with a ping pong paddle, and at that moment I expected my second whipping.

But she surprised me and said, "That is your sister."

"My sister?"

"Yes. She died when you were a baby."

Her name, I learned, was Alice, and she had died at age fourteen, in October 1935, when I was two years old. We were living across from the Little American Lunch at the time.

Mother also told me we had stopped being Catholic following her death.

Alice and I, mother told me, used to share the same bedroom. Alice had a heart condition which required her to take a medication. Medicine in those days came in little bottles with cork stoppers. It just so happened there was a similar bottle in the same medicine cabinet with carbolic acid in it, which Mother had been mixing with water and using to clean my eyes, as was the recommended practice back then. Alice took the wrong bottle. According to the doctor, the shock of the carbolic acid to her system could have stopped her heart. Mother figured Alice must have been feeling discomfort in her chest and rushed to get her medicine. In the dark, she picked up the wrong bottle.

But the Catholic Church refused to bury her, saying she had committed suicide.

This entire episode added another layer to my already complex religious life, which I'll get to, but it also opened up another window on my intriguing family background.

My mother's father, Joseph F. Kriss, was born in Germany in July 1848. He died in 1929 at the age of 81. I've never been able to find any documentation on his birth or immigration, but my aunt Edna Schneidt, Momma's sister, once told me he had been married earlier in Germany and had two sons. Not much else is known about those sons. By occupation, Granddaddy Kriss was a tailor.

My mother's mother, Katie Marie Kriss, was born in Budapest, Hungary, in March 1868. Her mother was a Gypsy. She came over to America to visit relatives in Chicago, and shortly after her arrival, there was news of a strong earthquake in Hungary that wiped out the little town where most of her family lived. She learned everyone in her family was killed. As a result, she never went back home.

How she met Joseph Kriss in not clear. He was 20 years older than her. Neither of them spoke English at the time and both spoke a different mother tongue. Somehow they managed to communicate in another Slavic language and over time added their own idiosyncratic words and phrases to be able to better converse with each other. They were living in New Jersey when my mother was born in 1901 and given the name Margaret. Shortly thereafter, they moved down to Charleston, South Carolina, and landed a contract with the Citadel military academy sewing buttons on the uniforms the cadets wore. So they had their own business for many years, working out of the basement of their home. A younger daughter, Edna, was born about eight years after my mother.

Mother told me that when she started school she knew little English, having mostly grown up with the mishmash language her parents spoke to each other. School started out as a scary experience for her as a result. She told me how every day when she came home from school, she would teach whatever English she had learned during the day to her mother and father. Slowly, with the added help of an African American woman they hired as a maid, they all acquired some proficiency in the English language, though Grandmother always spoke with a heavy accent.

Meanwhile, my grandparents must have done well sewing buttons onto uniforms. They did it for years. In those days, there were no zippers, and buttons were used for the fly on men's pants. Mother said those buttons had to be sewn on in a certain way so a man could just take a finger and run it down the line of buttons to undo them all. I used to think those buttons would have to come undone quickly or men had best not ever be in a hurry.

At age sixteen, in 1917, Mother married a young fellow who was in the navy. I learned about this later from my mother's sister, Aunt Edna, who used to have a photo of my mother and her first husband, dressed in his navy uniform. In 1919 the ship he was on was out on a six month cruise and virtually the whole ship came down with the influenza that created such a devastating pandemic during that period. Over half the sailors on board died before the ship arrived back at port in Charleston. Mother's first husband was among the dead, and she was already pregnant with Alice.

About a year later Mom met Dad, a man with a tragic background. He was always a bit secretive about where he had come from.

I used to say to him, "Daddy, don't you know when and where you were born?"

And he would reply, "Yeah, but I'll never tell."

The story I gathered in bits and pieces over the years was of a teenager coming to America after a terrible childhood trauma. His parents may have been quite wealthy, even aristocratic. The family name, Hadgopoulos,

Photo taken on a trip to my ancestral homeland in 1988. We are shown here with my Greek cousin, Dr. Demetrious Hadgopoulos, his wife Dr. Litsa Hadgopoulos, and son Pericles. Both Demetrious and Litsa are on the staff at the University of Crete.

meant landowner. They were large landholders near Smyrna, Turkey, living in a two story house, with expansive olive orchards and flocks of sheep and goats. I learned later my father had fourteen brothers and sisters, with two sets of twins in the family.

The region of Turkey where they lived was controlled by Greece at the time, though the territory was still in dispute, due to ongoing conflicts between Greece and Turkey. When Daddy was about fifteen years old, the Turkish military forces swept through the region in an attempt to retake the territory. They came at night and woke everyone in the family up, dragging them out to the front of the house. There, in front of all the children, Turkish soldiers beheaded my grandfather and raped and murdered my grandmother. The children were chased off, and they scattered along a creek running through the property and hid in an old culvert.

In the weeks following these murders, the children somehow managed to get back to Greece, where they had relatives near Lamia, which is about ninety miles northwest of Athens.

About a year later, in 1907, members of the extended family pooled resources to send my father to America. He was about sixteen at the time and was either the oldest or second oldest among the siblings. It is possible he also found a relative or family friend in America to sponsor him in exchange for a few years of work. I'm not really sure how the transition occurred.

He came by way of England, where he boarded a ship heading for America. When registering at the immigration office, he was asked what his name was, and he replied, "Hadgopoulos."

The agent writing down the information looked up at him and in a gruff voice said, "Hodges," and motioned with his hands to his lips for Daddy to repeat what he had just said.

Daddy told us how he repeated the name correctly, "Hodges," and how from then on he had an English name, which never seemed to bother him. Anglicizing names was pretty common back then, or people might just shorten their names to make them easier to pronounce. My father had learned enough English to know his given name, Demetrius in Greek, translated as James in English, and his middle name, Yodia, translated as George. That is how he became known as James George Hodges. His nickname was Jim.

He told us that he came to New York and started working in restaurants early on. Later he moved down to Savannah, Georgia, and continued supporting himself by working in restaurants, obviously picking up cooking skills as he went along. From Savannah, he moved to Charleston, which is where he met my mother. They were both having a good time at a community dance in the square, with a band playing under the gazebo. Daddy always loved to dance, and Mother said he was a pretty handsome, suave character at the time. He spoke with a bit of an accent but he was easy to understand. He must have taken a liking to the pretty, young widow he danced with—the one with long, tightly braided hair that stretched down to below her waist.

A few days later when he went by her home, she wasn't there; and her mother didn't like what she saw and chased him off with a broom. Grandmother didn't like him from the start; she thought he was older than he was saying. Undeterred, he came back, courting my mother and becoming acquainted with her little daughter, Alice. They were wed in 1921.

After the marriage, they moved to Rock Hill, South Carolina where my oldest brother, George, was born. Shortly thereafter, disaster struck, when the duplex they were living in burned to the ground. Daddy was at work, and Mother told me she was out in the park with her children the afternoon the house was destroyed. They lost everything. They ended up in Matthews, just southeast of Charlotte for a few years afterward, before moving into downtown Charlotte, where Daddy went into business for himself and opened the Little American Lunch.

I was born during the period of time when Daddy had the Little American Lunch.

Chapter Five

DEALING WITH DADDY

We had a healthy fear of Daddy. And as he grew older he grew even more unstable. I didn't learn until much later what had happened to him as a young boy back in Turkey, and perhaps the violence he witnessed there might explain, in part, his behavior later in life. But as a young child, I witnessed a disturbing amount of violence coming from my father.

When I was six years old, I was sitting at a back table in the restaurant eating a meal, as our family almost always took meals in Daddy's restaurant. Daddy had a young African American fellow, about nineteen years old, working for him as a dishwasher. An argument erupted between this young fellow and Daddy over pay. I heard Daddy say, "No, I paid you."

The next thing I saw was this young fellow backing Daddy up, and Daddy was saying, "Stay away from me. I don't want to hurt you."

He was backing Daddy toward the grill, and just as Daddy came up against it, the young man lunged for one of the knives by the cutting board next to the grill. I watched this all happen right before my eyes. Daddy was faster than him, obviously anticipating his move. Daddy had a hold of a knife in a split second, bringing it up from below just as the guy grabbed another knife. I didn't see the incision that ran up the young fellow's abdomen, all the way to his mouth. I just saw him suddenly bend over, then he ran past me into the street. Almost everyone in the restaurant chased after him.

When they caught up with him down at the corner, he had crumpled onto the curb. Someone called the police and a medic. Before they got him to the hospital he had died from loss of blood.

It was a clear case of self-defense, but not everyone saw it that way. A couple of days later Mother came to me and told me, "Don't you go anywhere without me. Do not leave the restaurant or go anywhere else."

Soon after, the police arrived in the restaurant and questioned witnesses. I overheard Leroy telling the police, "They better not harm that child. They better not come near that child."

Suddenly, I felt everyone was talking about me. I started crying and asking, "What's wrong?"

Then in walked an older black man, who I later learned was the father of the young man Daddy had knifed. He pointed right at me and said, "You better not let that child out of your sight, because it's going to be an eye for an eye, a child for a child."

Leroy popped around from back in the kitchen. "That child is going nowhere on this street without me," he shot back. You're going to have to take me out before you ever come close to this child. Now if you want a fix with me, you just come on and do it now."

That was the end of the matter. The old man walked out and I never heard another thing about him.

I never felt my father's actions in that incident were anything but justified. But the violence was disquieting nonetheless. And there was more. My oldest brother caught a lot of hell from my father. I remember one incident when George was about sixteen, not long before he joined the service. Mother and I were going up to our apartment when we saw Daddy at the top of the stairs really beating George. I stood there in horror, having never seen anything like it before. Mother was horrified as well. She could never understand why Daddy had such hostility toward George, who looked so much like our daddy.

Of course, George was more than a bit of a hell raiser himself. He ran around with three or four friends during high school. They were real rascals, always getting into things. They didn't go out and steal or

George in the U.S. Army, 1942.
(courtesy of Efird's Dept. Store, Charlotte, N.C.)

anything like that, but when we lived on College Street, he learned how to climb down the drainpipe at night from his upstairs bedroom, and he would run around with his friends, then climb the drainpipe back up to his bedroom window and return to bed. His activities went undetected until one night when he climbed the drainpipe up to the roof to play around. Coming back down, he got halfway down and the drainpipe broke. He had to scream for help and ended up getting a beating for sneaking out.

I think George and his friends used to sneak liquor, which was a popular thing for teenagers to do back then. And there was one time when he took Daddy's car without permission and went joyriding with his friends. He ended up getting a ticket for hot-rodding around town, and the police officer reported the incident to Daddy. George got into trouble big time for that.

Years later he told me about some of the other things he did together with his rebel friends. He thought it was all pretty funny.

I didn't agree, and told him, "It explains a lot of things."

I could see my father, with his European background and notions about authority, having to deal with a kid who was always getting himself into one form of trouble or other. I also came to understand the "mirror effect." When people see things in other people that they do not like, it is, more often than not, a trait they have in themselves. I think Daddy had to suppress a lot of rebelliousness in order to succeed. But it would surface when George acted out.

On December 9, 1941, two days after the Japanese attack on Pearl Harbor, George and three or four of his hell-raising friends all joined the Army together. For George, I think it was a chance to get away from the father he absolutely hated more than it was any patriotism on his part.

George was real honest with me, saying he might never come back. Hearing his words as an eight-year-old was pretty traumatic for me. He must have figured he'd probably be killed in the war and, if not, he would find someplace else to settle, away from his father. When he left home a week after signing up, he had no intention of ever coming back.

Alfred dressed in his Catholic school uniform, 1939. *(courtesy of Efird's Dept. Store, Charlotte, N.C.)*

With my brother Alfred, the relationship with our father was different. My mother always pampered him and wouldn't let our father touch him. She didn't want Alfred to have to suffer what George endured. Alfred wasn't a hell raiser, but he wasn't the most helpful person either. He could think of more ways to get out of doing chores than anybody I've ever known. He'd say, "My side hurts" or "My stomach hurts" or "I've got a headache." I remember the responsibility shifting to me so many times when he would do his act. I would end up being assigned to bring the coal into the house and empty the basin under the icebox where the melting ice water would drip.

I mostly escaped my father's wrath, but there were a few exceptions, one which left me embarrassed for years afterward. We were never allowed to drink Coca-Cola or any of the other soft drinks served in the restaurant. With Coke it was probably because in the early days there was actually a bit of cocaine in the recipe, and Daddy didn't want us ingesting that stuff. It may also have been a money thing. The more costly food served in the restaurant was reserved for paying customers. When we came in to get our meals, we ate what was left over and drank water and milk or buttermilk.

Just a few days after George signed up to go into the Army and before he left, Daddy decided to have a going away party for him. He told George he could invite his friends, and Daddy invited other family friends to the restaurant. This was when we were still living on College Street. By then an old storage room upstairs had been cleared out, opening a stairway that led directly from the restaurant up into the apartment we lived in.

The party was in full swing downstairs when a dear friend of my mother's, who we called Aunt Elsie, stopped me upstairs and asked, "Don't you want a Coca-Cola?"

"I can't have one," I said.

To which she replied, "Why not?"

"Because Daddy says we can't have Coca-Cola."

"Oh, I'll fix that," she said.

In a little bit she came back in the room carrying a bottle of Coke and sat down and said to me, "This is my Coca-Cola, but I'm going to let you have some of it."

Of course, I was thrilled to death, because I figured I wouldn't have to lie and say I hadn't had any. It seemed like a brilliant solution to me. I sat in her lap and started to enjoy my first Coke ever.

Wouldn't you know, Daddy walked in the room as I was sitting there sipping on that bottle of Coke. He walked right across the room toward me and grabbed the bottle out of my hand.

Aunt Elsie protested, "Jim, that's my Coca-Cola."

"I don't care," he said. "She knows she is not supposed to drink Coca-Cola."

He took me by the arm, lifted me up out of her lap, dragged me across the floor and down the stairs into the restaurant packed with people. Then he reached around my waist with one arm and raised me up and whacked me a good three or four times on the fanny, before Elsie and others intervened, telling him to stop. There I was, dressed up for a party in my fancy skirt and embarrassed to death in front of everyone. Needless to say, I didn't drink another Coke for years afterward.

Daddy was a fearful presence in my life, particularly when I was young. But I learned how to deal with him, and doing so was probably one of the more important skills I learned early in life. Rarely could I question his authority directly. Yet I learned to get along with him, to work for him, and to stand up for myself.

Once I started helping in the restaurant, I became his "baby girl" and his best worker. If he asked me to do something I didn't want to do, I would just say, "No, Daddy, I'm not going to do that." I wouldn't argue with him.

He used to tell me I should marry a Greek when I grew older. I was probably about fifteen by then. I just told him, "Daddy, I've been raised by a Greek, and there ain't no way I'm going to marry a Greek."

Mother thought he was going to take my head off right then and there, but he just laughed. He also told me I was the only one who could stand up to him respectfully.

There was one exception this, and it led to my first visit to a confessional at the Catholic Church. Daddy and I got into an argument at home. I'm not sure what it was about, but back then I did at times have a firecracker temper. Mother wasn't home and Daddy was drinking a beer. We were in the kitchen area where there was a table in the corner with built-in benches along the walls. He kept needling me until I blew, and when I did I picked up his bottle of beer and threw it at him.

The second I did it, I realized I had to get the hell out of Dodge, and the only place I could get where he couldn't reach me was down underneath the dinette set built into the corner. I huddled in the corner while he tried to reach in and get a hold of me.

Unable to reach in far enough, he finally started laughing and left. I don't know what he was saying as he walked out the room, but it sounded like, "Wait till I get my hands on you."

The whole episode frightened me so much that I went to my first confession to seek absolution for the guilt I felt. Once in the confessional I told the priest how I had become angry with my father and picked up a bottle of beer and thrown it at him. On the other side of the curtain I heard the priest make some strange noise. I asked, "Father, are you okay?"

He replied, "Yep. Just one question before I give you absolution. Did you hit him?"

I had to tell the truth. "No, I missed."

And then I heard a very distinct laugh. He went on to tell me, "Katherine, if that is the worst thing you ever do you are in good shape."

To which I answered, "Yeah, but I was really mad and really wanted to hit him with that bottle."

Then he asked, "Did he ever come back at you?"

And I told him, "No, he never did."

I excelled at O'Donahue High School in Charlotte, though I didn't always get along with the nuns, 1950.

Chapter Six

YOUNG AND SPIRITUALLY QUESTING

*Y*ears later Aunt Edna told me about my baptism in the Greek Orthodox Church, saying, "I just knew they were going to kill you."

In the Greek Orthodox tradition people are baptized by fully immersing them in water, whether they are infants or adults. I was baptized when I was about six months old at a ceremony attended by family members. The priest held me up in the air and pronounced, "In the name of the Father," then dipped me under the water. I came up screaming at the top of my lungs.

"And in the name of the Son," and under I went again, gurgling, emerging with another terrified scream for mercy. "And in the name of the Holy Ghost," with the same result. Aunt Edna said she had to get up and leave. She couldn't stand it.

Religious loyalties were mixed and ambiguous from the start in our family. My maternal grandmother knew where she stood, even if a Catholic priest in Brooklyn slighted her and kept her away from the church for several years. She was faithful in going to Mass most of her life. My father wanted very much to be loyal to his Greek Orthodox heritage, but his patience with the priests grew thin sometimes. Mother took Alice to the Catholic Church to be baptized before she met my father. My oldest brother George was baptized in the Greek Orthodox Church. Alfred, however, was baptized a Catholic. And I was baptized in the Greek Church.

After Alice died, and the Catholic priest at St. Peter's Catholic Church refused to perform her funeral, alleging she had committed suicide, Daddy was livid. A few weeks later there was some prominent citizen in Charlotte who jumped off what was then the tallest building in town, fourteen stories up, I believe it was. A high Mass funeral was performed for him in the Catholic Church the following Sunday. Mother and Daddy both said that was it. Daddy never went back to Mass at the Catholic Church.

By then Daddy had become involved more and more in a Greek civic organization called the American Hellenic Educational Progressive Association (AHEPA). We used to go the Greek Church on special holidays, —Easter, Christmas and such. But most of the time we went to Sunday school and church services at the nearby Presbyterian church. Mother would generally take us, and Daddy attended once in a while. We were living downtown at the time.

When we moved out to Kenilworth, I had two neighborhood friends who went to the Methodist church. Since the downtown Presbyterian Church was a long ways away for me, I started going to the Methodist church with my friends.

All dressed up to attend a wedding at the Greek Orthodox Church, around 1945. *(photo courtesy of Efird's Dept. Store, Charlotte, N.C.)*

After my grandmother came to live with us, she asked me to go to Mass with her. Mother was sure Daddy would kill me if he found out about it. Even Grandmother warned me, "Don't tell your Daddy."

I knew better than to tell my Daddy. But since Daddy was at work early Sunday morning, I went. That is my first recollection of being in a Catholic Church service.

Following my grandmother's death, my mother became concerned about Alfred and I having to go as far as we did to school and not having anyone at home when we arrived back in the afternoons. The O'Donahue Catholic School was just up the road from our home. I think Grandmother had long wanted to reconnect us to the Catholic Church and may have influenced Mother some before she died, but the reasons given had to do with our safety. We were enrolled in the school, but did not get involved in the church; otherwise Daddy would not have approved.

I started at the Catholic school when I began junior high. The seventh and the eighth grades were in the same classroom. I remember being a bit disappointed with the academic side of schooling, partly because I'd had some great teachers in my fifth and sixth grade in public school who were hard to match. But the spiritual side of the experience quickly began to capture my imagination.

I was so full of questions. I'd go over to the church and sit in a pew and be caught up in wonder. Memories of my grandmother flooded back. I'd look up at the statues of Jesus and the Blessed Mother and become enamored with the experience.

I fell in love with the Catholic Church, but I knew not to say anything because of my daddy. He was okay with my going to Catholic school; he just didn't want me to have anything to do with the Catholic Church.

Surreptitiously, I started getting up on Sunday mornings and going to mass at the Catholic Church after Daddy had left for work. Then I'd head over to the Methodist church to attend Sunday school, as well as the worship service. That way if my father inquired whether I went to church and what went on at church, I wouldn't have to lie to him about it. And if he wasn't going to be home on Sunday evening, I'd go to early Mass and to novena. I don't think Daddy ever knew about it.

As enraptured as I was with all the religious experience, perhaps it is no surprise that by the time I was in the eighth grade I had decided I wanted to become a nun. Some subtle encouragement to pursue a spiritual vocation was coming from the nuns and priests at school as well. And a number of the nuns thought my new commitment was just wonderful.

I told my mother, and she immediately said, "Oh please don't mention it to your father. Please don't."

I felt bolder, saying, "Well, Mother, he has to know, because it is what I am going to do. I am going to become a nun." This was all before I knew of my sister's death and what happened afterward.

It wasn't until near the end of my eighth grade year that I told Daddy my plan. He was in a particularly good mood one evening, telling me how proud he was of me to be graduating from the eighth grade. He was looking forward to the ceremony, with me wearing a cap and gown, and he said he was glad to see me going into high school.

That is when I dropped on him word of my ambition to become a nun.

His reaction was as expected, though he didn't hit me. But he did go ballistic. He was going to go over and blow up the church himself, absolutely. And all his prejudices spilled out.

"Go over to the convent and they will show you the tunnel that goes over to the rectory. The priests and the nuns all sleep around with each other. Do you know why they have graveyards in Catholic churches?" And on and on. Oh, he was mad at me. But I'd heard it all from him before.

I told him, "Daddy, I'm not even going to discuss it with you." And I never did discuss it with him; and he never brought it up again.

He need not have worried. By the time I was halfway through ninth grade, my desire to become a nun had already begun to wane. I still loved being close to the Church. I loved the holy sacrament. I felt it was a privilege when asked to help get the priest's robes ready, all laid out for him before the service. I'd help trim the candles and clean the altar. All that to me was very sacred. But I began to get the feeling there was more to life, more to

see and learn and do to help others than I would have access to in some convent. I also started hanging out with my peers more.

Some of my better friends at O'Donahue left to go to high school at Central High, a public school. O'Donahue only offered a limited sports program, and many of the guys wanted to play football and basketball. Even after they left, I'd still see them and hang out with some of them. One of the boys had a car. I remember he had an old screwdriver he used to shift gears with. About six of us would pile in his car and take off to football games at Central High or wherever the fun was. That was about as close to dating as I got in high school. You could call it double dating or triple dating. Few of my friends dated steady.

Of course, Daddy never knew about most of it. When guys would come to our home to see me, if it was in the afternoon when Daddy was home for a nap, he would come out in his undershorts with no shirt on and run the kids off. Or if Daddy was home when some guy would stop by to pick me up in the evening, Daddy would just embarrass me and the young man by telling him what he could do and what he better not do, and what Daddy would do if the young fellow did do it. What a horrible scene he would make.

I was also captain of the girl's basketball team, though it wasn't much of a team, and we always got beat when we played other schools. I was voted the most athletic girl in my graduating class. So I was socially active. I didn't feel like I was in a parochial environment, shut away in a convent. I knew what was going on in the world. The camaraderie I felt with my friends gave me an added incentive to think twice about becoming a nun.

I was voted the most athletic girl in my graduating high school class in 1951. Here I am with Don Williams, who was the most athletic boy.

And though there were a couple of nuns I really admired and saw as role models, there were others who gave their vocation a bad image. The way some of them behaved probably had more than anything else to do with my changing my mind about becoming a nun. There was one nun who carried on a vendetta against me for several years. I'm not sure what got it started, but she thought I was a negative influence on some of the postulants, the younger teachers who had recently joined the order. I used to help some of the postulants teaching first and second grade children.

There was one amusing incident where my nemesis was looking for me, suspecting I was helping this postulant teach her class. I knew she was after me, so when I arrived at the postulant's class, I told her about the nun looking for me. "She is really going to get me in big trouble if she finds me."

The young postulant, who was my soul-mate, replied, "She is not going to find you."

Facing the class, she told the young students, "Now children, we are going to play a little game. It's going to be really important how we play this game. Katherine is playing hide and seek and it is really important that she not be found, otherwise she will lose the game. So we are not going to lie when Sister comes in looking for her. We are going to be polite, yet not tell her."

Near the front of the class was a cloakroom, open on both ends. I ducked in there. Not long after, the nun came in, asking about me. The children all stood and said politely, "Good afternoon Sister." She started looking around, and as she did, I moved to one side and then the other of the cloakroom. I was sure one of the kids would give me away. About the time she was going to start questioning the students, the bell rang announcing time to change classes. The young postulant immediately said, "Children, it is time to gather your books and go to the next class."

I was mouthing "Thank you" to the students as they left, and a bunch of them replied "Yeah!" while the teacher kept saying "Shhhhh!" I didn't get caught.

But my little feuds with some of the nuns continued much of my way through high school and made for some miserable experiences. The same nun I had hid from also chased me through the hallways with scissors in her hand one day after school had been let out. I ran to the principal's office for protection.

Then at one point I was preparing to play a leading role in the school drama. As I recall, it was "Here Comes Charlie." I was playing Francis Miller. The nun directing the play had strict rules about not missing practice. This led to a conflict for me when my brother Alfred was going to graduate from Marine boot camp at Parris Island in South Carolina, and his wife wanted me to accompany her down to his graduation.

With my sister-in-law, Janet Gettier Hodges, in 1950. I was 16.

I made the effort of getting permission from the school principal to miss school on Friday, and I let the drama teacher know I'd have to miss one practice session. I knew my part well, even though the performances were still several weeks away. She wasn't pleased, and scheduled a dress rehearsal for Friday, saying anyone who missed it was out of the play.

I went ahead and attended my brother's graduation and pleaded with the drama teacher afterwards, but to no avail. Not only was I kicked out of the play, she told me I would fail the drama class as well. I had to appeal to the Monsignor to get her overruled on the latter. The whole experience left me pretty angry, and I told her that there is no way in the world I would want any part of being a nun after witnessing her behavior.

There were nuns who pressured me to change my mind and re-think becoming a nun. And I was amazed at how nuns turned against me once they found out I wasn't going to be heading the way they thought

I should. But not all of them were so insensitive. There was one nun who joined the order in her thirties, so she had plenty of experience being in the real world. During a discussion in class one day about what we planned to do for careers, she turned to me and said, "Katherine, I understand you are going to be a nun."

The other students all giggled, then one of the guys said, "You haven't told her Katherine, have you?"

And that is when I really made it official. "No," I said. "I'm not going to become a nun. I'm going to do something in business and probably get married."

I was a bit stunned by her response, when she replied, "That is okay."

I remember her name was Sister Michelle, and I appreciated her affirmation of my decision.

Altogether I think I received a pretty good education at O'Donahue. I excelled in Spanish, enough to get a job doing translation work after just one year. I took Algebra I and II, which was the most that was offered in mathematics. When we were tested during our senior year for physical and mental dexterity, I was told the results showed I would always be really good with finance, money and anything having to do with machines. At graduation two types of diplomas were awarded: General diplomas meant you had met all the state standards; academic diplomas signified college preparation, with training in math, a foreign language and other advanced courses. I had earned an academic diploma.

But besides academics, there was one other side to my high school education. I enrolled in many of the religion classes offered, eager to learn and to understand. I was searching and I wasn't content with learning the catechism by rote. As a result I asked a lot of questions. I also had contrasting experiences to draw from—things I had learned attending the Presbyterian, Methodist and Greek Orthodox churches. I wanted to know why the priests didn't preach from the Bible and so much else.

These classes were generally taught by priests. One of them once asked me if I was Catholic. I responded, "No, but that doesn't mean I don't want to learn."

Graduation from high school in 1951 *(photo courtesy of Franklin Studios, Charlotte, N.C.)*

"Quit asking so many questions," he said.

To which I replied, "Well, how are we ever going to learn anything if we don't raise questions?"

Some of the guys in the class jumped in at that point, saying, "Yeah, go for it, Katherine."

The priest dismissed the smart alecks from the class, but let me stay. I saw him later in the hallway and told him, "I wasn't trying, Father, to cause problems, but there are a lot of non-Catholics like me who are coming here, and if you can't answer our questions…"

His reply only left me half satisfied. He said he didn't like smart alecks, but "I didn't catch from you that you were being a smart aleck. Just don't ask any deep questions."

How could I not ask deep questions? And if the priests weren't going to give me satisfactory answers, I'd have to look elsewhere.

Chapter Seven

LEARNING TO LOVE WORK

While growing up, I never thought about work as a nine-to-five activity. My father was up before six in the morning, six days a week, and off to work. He came home to rest a bit in the afternoon, and then he worked until nine or ten at night. I took such work habits for granted, thinking everyone should work that way. Work was what people did when they were awake.

What's more, from an early age work seemed like so much fun to me. Starting when I was about five years old, Daddy started putting me to work in the restaurant. He'd sit me up on the counter by the cash register. When someone paid his bill with a quarter or a fifty-cent piece, Daddy would tell me to count out the required change. I learned all about money and making change.

To Daddy, I was always "Katina" or "Kat" or "Baby Girl." The latter always made me feel like the apple of his eye.

A year or two later I was given the job of seating customers when things got busy. I would show them to their tables and give them menus and say, "Someone will be with you in a minute."

Soon I was bringing customers their water and laying out the silverware for them. Of course I heard a lot of comments about "How cute she is," which just made it all the more wonderful for me. Once a couple of Army officers came in with their wives. I seated them. The place was busy, so someone told me to take their order. That was my first order, a real novelty for them and me. I wrote down their order and took it back to Daddy, then delivered their drinks and set out napkins and knives and forks for them. Someone else brought the order out, but when they left, there was a fifty-cent tip on the table for me. I was elated, until Daddy took the tip.

By the time I was ten and eleven years old, I was working regularly in the restaurant after school and on weekends. I became good at it and would always make more money on tips than the other waitresses, which led to complaints. They thought I was being favored with better stations. So Daddy moved me to the worst stations. But still I came out ahead, and Daddy moved me again. He started getting impatient with the issue.

Then one day on my twelfth birthday, five or six guys from the Belk's maintenance department came in. I knew these customers, and they always wanted to sit in my section. I had been letting customers know all day long that it was my birthday and I was getting some extra big tips. They sat in my section, and I was taking their orders when, all of a sudden, Daddy screamed at me from the kitchen. I had forgotten someone's bread order or something.

I started to head back to the kitchen, saying to the guys, "I'll be right back."

But one of the fellows caught me and asked, "Does he yell at you like that all the time?"

I sort of nodded sheepishly and said, "Yeah."

So this guy stands up and says to the others, "Come on guys, let's go."

I thought they were leaving, but they followed me to the kitchen. I was scared to death of what was going to happen next.

When they came face to face with Daddy in the kitchen, one of them said, "Jimmy Hodges, you ever yell at this young lady again, we will never come back to your restaurant." Then they all turned around and walked out of the kitchen and sat back down at their table.

And Daddy turned to me and politely asked, "Would you mind taking this bread out to the table? Please."

He never yelled at me again in the restaurant after that.

But it didn't solve the issue of other waitresses complaining about me getting more tips. Daddy moved me again, and finally he told me,

"I'm taking your tips and splitting them with the other waitresses. I'm losing them."

To which I simply replied, "In that case, I'll just go find a job somewhere else."

"You'll never find a job elsewhere," he snarled.

I guess he underestimated me. I was thirteen by then, still too young to be in the employment market. Mother was working at Belk's at the time and she talked to her boss. The question of my age came up and Mother told her I looked sixteen. Her boss said, "Okay, but you'll have to get by the Department of Labor."

Mother took me downtown to the Department of Labor and signed a consent form saying I could work. And I went to work at Belk's department store in the "tube room" upstairs, where orders and payments were sent from different areas on the floor by being sucked through tubes in little capsules. Since Belk's back then only stayed open late one night a week, Friday, and didn't open on Sunday, and I had to go to school during the

Around the time of my graduation from high school in 1950.

47

day, it was really just a part-time job for me Friday afternoons and nights, and Saturdays.

After a year in the tube room, I was transferred down onto the floor and given the responsibilities of a cashier. I worked in that position for two years. Meanwhile, I also started to learn about wage discrepancies, hearing how Sears department store paid more. I was only getting about forty cents an hour at Belk's, but I wasn't sure anyone else would hire me while I was still under sixteen.

When my sixteenth birthday rolled around, I thought, "Now I can get a real job."

I got all dressed up on my birthday to go to work at Belk's. It was a Saturday, which couldn't have been more perfect. I did my makeup and hair, and I wore my heels. The manager couldn't help but notice me. He came over and inquired, "Katherine, what is the special occasion? You are all dressed up today."

"Sixteen," I said.

"What?" he blurted out.

No one under sixteen was supposed to be working there, and I'd been there nearly three years.

Then I added, "And I put my notice in today and I'm leaving in two weeks."

Of course he wanted to know where I was going, and I said, "Sears."

He gave me an affirmative reply: "I don't blame you." He knew the difference.

I started out making seventy-five cents an hour at Sears.

A year later I transferred over to the old Bank of Charlotte. They were pretty impressed with my resume: four years working in department stores, three as a cashier, and as a waitress before that, plus an academic diploma from high school. And I was only seventeen, the younger of only two female tellers working at the bank. I was still working at the bank when I first met a young marine named Ron Harper.

Chapter Eight

MOTHER, FATHER, AND I

My mother once told me she prayed me into this world. She prayed for a baby girl, because Daddy said he would not let her stop being pregnant until he had a girl.

Of course I wanted to know why it was so important for him to have a baby girl. And she said, "For some stupid reason Greek men believe they have to have a girl to prove their manhood. They want boys for the namesake, but they want at least one girl to be able to claim their manhood."

Much later when Ron and I traveled to my ancestral village in Greece and met relatives over there, I couldn't help but ask about this notion of men wanting baby girls. I was told, frankly, "Yeah, we still believe that."

Well, just how excited Daddy was to have a new baby girl was seriously questioned by mother and others in the family. I was informed of the details many years later after a strange turn of events.

I was probably in the sixth or seventh grade when I learned how one can give one's hair a special shine by putting lemon juice on it after washing it. I washed my hair one afternoon and then rubbed the lemon juice in as instructed. When my hair dried it had red highlights, which I thought looked cute.

When Mother came home and saw my hair she was furious. She really raised hell. I had never seen my mother so angry. She thought I had used henna or dyed my hair. She wanted to know, "What did you do to your hair?"

I told her I had just used lemon juice, but by then she had reduced me to tears. I had no idea why she was so incensed.

Years later my mother's good friend who we called Aunt Elsie came down to visit us. We got to talking about my mother. My father had passed away by then, and Aunt Elsie told me, "I'll tell you what happened the night you were born because your mother never will, but you need to know. It's part of what you should know."

She went on to relate how Daddy was out on a date with a redheaded woman the night I entered this world. I don't know how long this other woman was in his life, but it was long enough. Aunt Elsie said it just devastated my mother. The one thing Daddy wanted so badly was a baby girl, and here was Mother having this baby girl and he was out gallivanting around. Aunt Elsie told me how when he was finally dropped off by the woman, who had a car, and came in the house, she stood at the door with both hands on her hips and said, "Well, you finally got your little girl."

Daddy started past her, wanting to go in and see the mother and child. But Aunt Elsie stopped him short and told him, "You're not going near your wife or that baby until you are completely bathed." Daddy listened to her.

After telling me the story, Aunt Elsie reminded me of the red highlights in my hair. "Are you connecting now?" she asked.

From before I came into this world there was an uneasy relationship between my mother and my father. Daddy, no doubt, was the dominant figure in my childhood. But Mother was more of a confidant for me, though I often felt sorry for her for not being able to stand up for herself. She had a tough challenge, trying to keep the family together for the sake of the kids but also out of a fear of facing the unknown of life after a divorce.

I never saw my father hit my mother, never saw any physical cruelty. But fits of rage and threats were part of his personality. There was a lot of verbal abuse. Someone once asked me if I knew any Greek. I had to say, "Only the bad words, the ones I learned from my father." Over the years we kids learned what they all meant.

Daddy also deprived Mother of so much. She worked long hours as a waitress in the restaurants he ran, yet he controlled the purse strings. She would have to tell him what she needed to buy for the household, and he would dole out just what was required for the purchases and no more. If she took money without telling him and he found out about it, she would catch hell from him.

This became such a contentious issue that she finally consulted with an attorney. The attorney told her she had a right to half of what came in, and she should count out the money in the cash register and take half, leaving a note to let Daddy know what she had taken. The attorney promised to defend her if there was any more trouble. Daddy cooled off for awhile afterward, but still Mother, always fearful of a confrontation, remained reticent about taking money out of the register without seeking his permission to do so.

At home she made do. For a long time she washed clothes in a tub, using an old washboard. Later she did get an old style spinner washing machine. We had to put the clothes in a tub to soak overnight and then run them through the agitator on the machine before putting them through a wringer. Any stains would have to be scrubbed out on the washboard. The whole operation took a lot of water. Then, no matter what time of year it was, we hung everything out to dry. Washing clothes generally was an all-day job for my mother every Monday.

Long after refrigerators became affordable, we still had an icebox out on the back porch. We had to keep it out there because the pan that caught the melting ice would frequently overflow.

The furniture in the house was fancy enough—nothing but the best for Daddy—but when it came to things Mother needed to keep the household running, there never was money for those items.

With his suave style and expensive suits, Daddy fancied himself a ladies' man. He left Mother feeling insecure as a result. There was at least one other woman in his life who I became aware of. Mother told of finding a receipt in his suit pocket for a bunch of jewelry. But Mother also distrusted receiving gifts from Daddy, thinking he was just trying to keep her satisfied while he was jagging about on the side.

There was also plenty of harassment of waitresses in the restaurant. Women didn't quit working just because he didn't pay them enough or because I earned more in tips. Daddy's behavior finally started catching up with him when, on one occasion, a waitress lifted her leg up on a box to straighten her hose, and Daddy came up behind her and pinched her. She took him to court.

I don't think Mother knew anything about it until one day she and I were in the restaurant and a customer came in and said, "Well, Margaret, the judge really got Jim today."

"What judge?" she asked.

"Oh God, you didn't know," he blurted out. "Well, I might as well tell you. I was called in as a character witness for Jim, but it didn't do any good. The judge told Jim, this being the second time he was before the court on this kind of a charge, that if he saw him in again, Jim wouldn't see the inside of the jail, he'd be under the jail. So I don't think you are going to have any trouble with your waitresses anymore."

Not long after that incident, Aunt Edna began encouraging Mother to find her own employment and let Daddy run the restaurant business on his own. Aunt Edna was working at Belk's at the time in the tube room. This was shortly before I started working there. When another employment opportunity came along, she encouraged Mother to apply for the position.

At first Mother said, "Oh, Jim would kill me. I don't know if I could do that."

But Aunt Edna persisted. "No he won't. He might raise Cain but he won't kill you."

Mother was actually a very capable person. She played a big part in running a successful restaurant business all those years, as well as keeping a household together. Before she married Daddy, she had worked in a cigar factory down in Charleston. She ended up taking the job at Belk's and must have felt more than a bit liberated.

She saved up her money and bought needed items for the household. After all the years of slaving every Monday with the wash, she was proud to buy one of the new Westinghouse washer-and-dryer combination machines. She just had to put the clothes in the washer, and after the wash cycle, the drier would automatically come on and dry them. We still had to iron them, which was mostly my job. As soon as I was old enough to reach the ironing board, I started starching and ironing shirts and pants for everyone in the family. But Mom's life was made a whole lot easier with her new washer/drier.

Next she bought a new electric refrigerator, replacing the old, leaky icebox on the back porch. She was enjoying her financial independence and felt so tickled about spending her own money on things she really needed. But when Mother helped me get my worker's permit, and I started working at Belk's too, Daddy blew like a volcano.

"That's it, food on the table, roof over the head, that's it." He made it clear he wasn't going to pay for anything else. No more clothes out of his earnings, and certainly no tuition payments for a Catholic school education or piano lessons.

There was only one time when Daddy really scared me, and it was not long after Mother and I both started working at Belk's. We were at home one day when we heard Daddy pull his car into the carport. Mother mentioned something about not remembering what Daddy was angry about this time. I went to a little window and looked down into the carport and watched as Daddy reached over to the glove box and pulled out a handgun. As soon as I saw the gun, I ran and locked the door and closed and locked all the windows on the front of the house.

He came to the door and, unable to open it, demanded that we unlock it.

Trying to act calm, I said, "Daddy, I'm not going to open the door. I don't know what is wrong with you and I don't know why you are mad, but you are not coming in the house. We're not letting you in until you put the gun back in the car, otherwise we'll call the police."

He tried to argue for awhile, then added a few curses. He could have shot through the window. But he finally calmed down and put the gun away. We never learned what he intended to do that day.

Daddy was having a hard time in those days. Jim's Grill was a big success and he made plenty of money. But he always wanted something better, more than the diner kind of place with a counter and booths. He wanted something more upscale, a classy restaurant, one where his culinary skills could earn him a wider reputation.

When my parents first moved to Charlotte, Daddy worked as a food preparer and cook in the restaurant attached to the Barringer Hotel, on the corner of 5th and College Street. This same restaurant came up for lease later on, and Daddy saw the chance to fulfill his dream.

The whole restaurant had to be renovated. The hotel owners told him he could do anything he wanted, but it had to be his money and they would not reimburse him for his investment. He went and bought the wood and manufactured his own custom tables. He wanted his restaurant to have fancy tables and chairs; and when he finished the tables, the wood in them had such a shine you could see your face in them. There were also renovations to the kitchen. He wanted all stainless steel. He gave the place a real upscale atmosphere. And he was so proud when he had his grand opening.

He had spent a ton of money on getting the place ready. Mother was so upset and anxious. But he would reassure her, "Margaret, it's going to be okay."

The new restaurant turned into a two-year financial drain. Daddy had miscalculated regarding his local clientele. Most of the people living in the area around there were working people. He just couldn't attract the kind of customers he was after. Plus, he didn't have any reserves left after sinking so much into the renovation of the place.

He ended up going bankrupt. Mother worried that we would lose our home. But Daddy had hired a clever lawyer, who advised him in advance to transfer the ownership of the house to a cousin of his, someone I never met. We kept the house, but Daddy lost everything else he had and ended up working for other people for awhile, living out of town to get the kind of positions he wanted. The turmoil in his life took a toll on my parents' relationship.

I have often pondered my parents' marriage, wondering how it might have been different. I'd ask my mother, "Why do you stay with him?"

"For you children," she would reply.

Yet I never really believed that answer. After my older brothers left, I said to her, kind of tongue-in-cheek, "Well Mom, we're down to me," suggesting we could make it on our own.

And she would say, "Well, I don't know."

Then after I got married and left home, I told her, "Okay, now you are free." But of course, she wasn't going anywhere.

I didn't like her laying this burden on us kids, basically saying we were the reason she endured all the emotional pain and suffering she went through. It was more or less our fault that she had to stay with him. For some reason, I just didn't believe it.

She didn't think I could understand her situation. She thought Daddy favored me. The "my baby girl" talk when I worked in the restaurant would make her jealous. I was special in Daddy's eyes, in her view.

I couldn't disagree with her on the topic because she would say "Well, you wouldn't know how it feels to be in my position because you are so special to him."

I don't think Daddy ever did any more for me than he did for his sons. If anyone did more for particular children, it was Mother. She overcompensated for her sons when she thought their father was neglecting them. And she would justify it by saying, "Someday they will be taking care of me." Her thinking was that she would never have to worry as long as she had my oldest brother around. She really was into the old European tradition of the oldest son taking care of the mother. And she had no idea that I would be the one taking care of her at the end of her life.

Yet, I think there was more going on between my mother and me. Mother would get irritated at me for the way I would stand up to Daddy. Somewhere I learned to be assertive, and to do it in a way that didn't push Daddy over the edge to where he would get enraged. My mother used to say she didn't know where I got it from, but she obviously resented me for being able to do what she couldn't do. I wasn't intimidated by Daddy's anger like she was.

Even with Mother, I would ask for a justification if she made demands on me. If I wanted to go out and she said I couldn't, I'd be a bit stubborn and want to know why. I began to realize she trusted me less than my father did.

I have to conclude my mother put up with all the abuse she received from my father because of a basic fear. She didn't know what the alternative would be. She never felt confident she could make it on her own in the world without her husband. And I think it is so important for young women to learn to be able to take care of themselves before getting into a marriage. Otherwise, a woman can end up stuck between an abusive husband and a fear of not being able to make it on her own.

What is interesting is that later, when my father became really ill and needed a lot of help, Mother was there for him. I couldn't help but ask her "Why?"

"He needs me now," she said. "He never needed me before."

I had never thought about it in those terms. And I realized, for a relationship to be healthy, it is important that we need each other—not some particular need that can be easily discarded or fulfilled elsewhere, but a healthy need for one another.

Chapter Nine

"You are Concert Pianist Material"

I started taking piano lessons when I was in sixth grade and continued for seven years, until I became really good at playing. A college scholarship to Queens College was within reach for me. That was my goal, to win that scholarship by excelling on the piano.

My grandmother was the one who first arranged for me to take piano lessons. One of the sisters at the convent up the street taught me, and we had an old upright piano in the house, which I practiced on. Grandma loved to sit in her rocking chair and listen to me play. When Daddy came home for his afternoon naps I would stop, but as soon as he was out the door to go back to work, I was on the piano again. I'd keep playing until other family members came home in the evening.

When I started going to the Catholic school, I took lessons there for awhile. But I wasn't progressing as well as I thought I could, and someone suggested I take private lessons. A piano teacher named Ziggy Herwitz taught lessons out of his home, and he was willing to take me on as a student.

From the start, Ziggy thought I had real potential. He taught me so much, and I loved playing on his grand piano. After I had progressed further, he had me listen to records of piano pieces performed by concert pianists. Then he taught me how to emulate their styles. He urged me to practice, practice, practice, until I could play a piece just like it sounded on the record.

My piano skills kept improving. I got to where I could play those pieces absolutely perfectly. And after a couple of years working with Ziggy, he told me about the scholarship program at Queens College for pianists. A two-year scholarship was offered every year, and Ziggy thought I had a great chance of winning it.

"You are going to get this scholarship," he told me. "You are concert pianist material."

I was so excited. I started imagining myself spending two years at Queens. Then I figured I would be moving up to other opportunities on the way to a career playing at concerts. I practiced every opportunity I got, in the mornings, in the afternoons, during nearly all my spare time.

Daddy wasn't a big fan of mine. He wouldn't help pay for my lessons. Mother and I covered those out of our earnings. And though Daddy would let someone come in and tune the old upright piano I practiced on, he made it clear that if it ever broke down, he wasn't going to replace it. The piano would have to go.

I worked hard for three years, determined to win the Queens College scholarship. But during my senior year of high school, the strings on our old upright piano began to break. I would hit some keys and just get a thud. I tried to learn to work around the broken keys, but more began to fail. There was no getting around it. I had practiced so much I had basically worn the old piano out.

I have to say, Mother really argued my case that time. She went to bat for me, fussing at Daddy to get the piano fixed. He came back at me, telling me piano playing was a total waste of time.

Finally Daddy said, "I'll arrange to send someone out to the house."

We figured he was going to send someone out to pick up the piano and take it to get it fixed. Someone did come and get the piano, but it was the last we ever saw of it.

Daddy let it be known, "It's a waste of time. Now I'll hear no more about it."

Ziggy tried to help out. He offered to let me come over to his place in Dilworth and practice on his beautiful grand piano. But getting there and back was no easy matter, given my schooling and work schedule. I just cried.

The chance to go to college meant nothing to Daddy. He wanted me to graduate from high school, but to him, anything beyond high school

Still enjoying the keyboards on an organ Ron bought for me in 1960.

was unnecessary. He saw no value in it. And he had little room for the arts in his life.

When it came to piano playing, he said, "Only men can make money playing the piano. Look at concerts. Who do you see playing?"

He was right. All concert pianists back then were men. Even today, you seldom see women succeed on the concert circuit. Still, for me, just being able to get to that level of playing—to be able to succeed at something—was what was important.

I really had a tough time with Daddy afterward. He never understood how important it was to me. My heart was really broken. But Daddy was still mad at me and Mother for having deserted him at the restaurant and gone and taken jobs at Belk's department store.

Ron as a marine in his dress blues, 1951.

Chapter Ten

MEETING RONNIE

"**When you meet the man you are going to marry,** you will fall like a hot potato."

I wasn't sure what Grandmother meant, so I asked her, "What do you mean, hot potato?"

And she said, "Hot potato: out of the oven, into your hand, and swoosh, that is how you fall in love."

She was right.

Daddy had pretty much laid down the rules for the young guys who used to come pick me up to go out when I was still in high school. But after Daddy's restaurant went bankrupt, he lived away from home for a few years. He worked awhile at the Greensboro Country Club as a chef, then took a job at a restaurant in Myrtle Beach, and later worked in an eating establishment in Jacksonville, North Carolina, just outside Camp Lejeune, the U.S. Marine base.

I was delighted to have him out of town. I could lead my own life. And I did, at age seventeen, leaving my department store job at Sears and taking that position as a teller at the Bank of Charlotte. At the time I was the youngest teller and one of only two female tellers working at the bank. I was already on the road to success.

Daddy wasn't around to monitor my dating and lecture the young men about what they could and better not do, and Mother was always distrustful of me when it came to boys, figuring I wouldn't do the right thing. So I found myself relying on the wisdom my grandmother had instilled in me when I was a little girl. I can remember her telling me, "Play around, but don't do that."

I didn't even know what she meant by "play around." What she did get into my head, however, was that the greatest gift I could give my future husband was my virginity, and presenting my virginity to my husband was a beautiful act and the way God intended a marriage union to begin. Once Grandmother put the matter to me in those terms, that was it. Mother need not have worried.

My early dating experiences after high school were not promising. My brother Alfred was still in the Marines at Parris Island, South Carolina. His wife, Janet, and I used to go down together to visit him. And he started setting me up with dates, fellow marines, so he could go off and be alone with Janet.

The first marine I dated spent most of the evening talking about his girlfriend back home. I fell asleep on him. The next one I practically had to wrestle with to keep his hands off me. He kept trying to "put the make on me," as kids say these days. I told Alfred afterward I didn't want to date anymore marine "octopuses."

Meanwhile, Alfred was transferred up to Camp Lejeune and Janet moved into an apartment in nearby Wilmington. They invited me down for a visit. I told them not to bother lining up a date for me or I wouldn't come.

Nonetheless, Janet wrote to tell me about the marine corporal in command of Alfred's unit, how nice this man was and blah, blah, blah.

I thought, "there goes my brother again, trying to make points with his boss.

I called them and told them, "I'm not coming."

Janet wanted to know why.

"I don't want a date," I told her. "I'm coming down to visit the two of you and that is it."

So they said, "Okay." Alfred agreed to tell his corporal the planned date was off.

I took a day off work and left on a Friday morning, riding a bus down to Wilmington. When I arrived, Alfred was at the bus station to meet me.

Outside the front of our home on Kenilworth Avenue on the day of Alfred and Janet's wedding. From the left are my mother and father, my Aunt Edna, Janet, her new husband Alfred (my brother), and the matron of honor, me.

I took one step off the bus and he walked up and said to me, "Now Sis, don't get mad. I couldn't get in touch with him to cancel the date. Just date him tonight. Janet is fixing dinner at the apartment. We're going to have dinner and then go to a movie. It will be the last date you have with the guy."

I felt I had to concede, "All right, just tonight."

Ronnie came by at dinner time. He was a nice looking young man, dressed in his "civvies," not in his uniform. We had dinner, accompanied by pleasant conversation. Then we all went to a movie. Afterward Ronnie and I went for a long walk, arriving back at the apartment around midnight. We sat in the swing on the back porch and talked and talked, late into the night.

By then I already knew I was going to marry him, but I had the good sense not to tell him.

It was probably two o'clock in the morning when he finally said, "I guess I better start thinking about getting back to the base."

I was saying to myself, "I don't want this to be the last date with this marine." And I asked him, "Will I see you again?"

And he replied, "Yes, if when I get back, my buddy has remembered to wash my skivvies, I can come tomorrow."

I wasn't sure what he was talking about, but thought, "It must be something really important."

The next morning as Alfred was preparing to leave, I asked him to find out if Ronnie was going to be coming back.

"Oh, I have a feeling he'll be back," Alfred replied.

Then I had to ask, "Wait a minute. What are skivvies?"

Alfred laughed and wanted to know what would make me ask.

I said, "Because he said if his buddy had washed his skivvies he'd be back."

Alfred laughed again and then informed me, "That's his underwear."

In the evening Ronnie accompanied Alfred back to the apartment, and we had another pleasant time together. I was scheduled to leave the following day to go back to Charlotte, but Ronnie suggested I come by the base in the morning with Alfred before leaving.

We did go by the base in the morning. It was the first time I saw Ronnie in uniform. My God, he was so spit-and-polish it was incredible. There wasn't a wrinkle anywhere on his uniform except the creases along his pant legs, and you could have cut your finger on those. With a stocky build that filled out his uniform well, he looked so handsome.

We didn't have time for more than a few pleasantries before Ronnie had to leave for maneuvers up in Little Creek, Virginia. I handed him my address written on a slip of paper, and he wrote his out for me. I promised him I would write but wondered if I would see him again. He assured me I would.

We started corresponding, and I still have a treasure trove of all the letters we exchanged.

I really believe my meeting Ronnie was an answer to my prayers. I remembered what my grandmother had said, "When you meet the right man, you'll know; you'll fall like a hot potato."

I had also done a novena for two years leading up to our meeting, praying in the church to the Blessed Mother. The sole purpose of my prayers was asking direction in finding someone to share my life with. Meeting Ronnie and knowing right away he was the one just seemed like a natural consequence. I knew he was destined for me and I for him.

This was the first photo Ron and I had taken together, shortly after we met in August of 1951.

Chapter Eleven

COURTSHIP

We first met on August 3, 1951, and I didn't see Ronnie again for over a month. But Mother could sense something important was happening in my life.

She asked me one day, "You really liked the young man you dated in Wilmington, didn't you?"

"Yes, I did," I had to admit.

Not long after, Mother inquired again, saying, "You're in love, aren't you?"

I looked at her and said, "I believe so, Mother. But what made you think that was the case?"

"Because, generally when you go on dates, you come back and chatter all the time, telling me about where you went and what you did. This time you haven't said two words about the guy you dated since you got home. So I figured it must be pretty serious."

Ronnie was gone on maneuvers in Virginia for several weeks. We corresponded while he was away, deciding to meet again on Labor Day weekend.

Mother was getting more and more curious and asked if she could accompany me down to Wilmington and meet Ronnie. I let Ronnie know, and we made arrangements to stay in a little boarding house. When we arrived and I introduced Ronnie to my mother, she immediately liked him.

Not long after our second meeting we starting discussing getting married. Ronnie never actually proposed to me. The whole thing came about naturally. We just started discussing when would be the best time for us to get married. He was scheduled to be discharged from the Marines at the end of January, 1952, and we talked about getting married in February.

Of course I wanted Ronnie to meet my father before our plans got too advanced. Not that I was going to let Daddy influence my decision, but I had no idea how Daddy was going to react to news of my marriage plans, or what he would think of Ronnie.

As he grew older, Daddy had begun to change. His bad moods would last longer. We learned later that he was drinking more. I told Ronnie not to pay any heed to him if he acted disagreeable, because whatever Daddy said, his opinion was not going to sway me in any way.

By this time my father had moved to Jacksonville and taken a position as head chef and manager of a restaurant not far from the base where Ronnie was stationed. On my third visit down to the coast to visit with Ronnie, I took him by to meet my father, not knowing what would happen and bracing myself for the worst.

I did let Daddy know in advance we were coming. And I had even told him Ronnie and I were going to get married. So I was holding my breath when we approached the restaurant where Daddy worked.

Daddy saw us coming and met us at the front door. I hugged him and gave him a kiss, then introduced him to Ronnie. The next thing I knew, he put his arm around Ronnie and walked off and started introducing him to everyone in the restaurant, the waitresses and all the customers, leaving me standing at the front door with my mouth wide open. I couldn't believe it and I was imagining Ronnie would think everything I told him about my father was a lie.

Daddy took to him immediately. He really did. He came back to me and said, "Well, Katina, come on, I want everyone to meet you, too." I was still standing there amazed.

Then Daddy said to me, "Tell me just one thing. Tell me you are not marrying to spite or get away from me."

I looked at him and said in all sincerity, "Daddy, I would never do that to myself. No, I'm getting married because I really am in love with him." That was all I needed to say. Daddy was agreeable to everything from then on.

Ronnie started hitchhiking up to Charlotte on the weekends to see me. We began making arrangements for our wedding, even scheduling "instruction prior to marriage" sessions with the monsignor at the church. Ronnie took a ten-day leave for the marriage preparation sessions and stayed with Mother and me at our home.

The marriage preparation sessions were a bit of a joke. When the monsignor got to the part about sex, he said to me, "You do understand what the wifely duties are, do you not?"

When I replied, "Yes," we could see a sigh of relief come across his face. He wasn't going to have to go into any details with us.

Of course, I didn't know much, except for what my aunt—not my mother—had taught me.

Mother was the one who first suggested I needed to meet Ronnie's parents before the wedding. "When you marry the man, you marry the family," she said. "You need to know them, and they need to know you."

We all agreed it was a good idea.

Ronnie made a trip to visit his parents in Cumberland, Maryland, and asked his father if he could borrow his car to drive down to North Carolina, so he could use it to bring me with him to spend Christmas with the Harper family. The car was going to save a lot of time and hassle for us, not having to make train and bus connections.

But when Ronnie arrived in Charlotte to pick me up, Mother started having misgivings. She never did trust me much when it came to dating. She figured Ronnie and I weren't married yet and shouldn't be together so long in a car. But she wouldn't come out and say so. She reminded us that it was against the law in North Carolina for a young, underage, unmarried couple to go across the state line. She just knew we were going to be arrested.

I kept assuring her, "No, I'm sure he is a good driver. That won't happen."

Then she started insisting Daddy would not allow us to drive all the way up to Maryland together in a car.

"He won't allow you to go in the car. We didn't know you were going to go by car."

I tried to explain, "Mother, it is wonderful that we can drive straight through and not take so long to get there."

"He won't like it," she kept insisting. "And then I'll hear about it and everything."

"Mother," I told her, "it doesn't matter what he thinks."

Still, she came back with, "Well, I'm going to call your daddy and tell him, and you know he won't want you to go."

She went in and called him on the telephone. I could hear her talking to him in a very excited voice. "Jimmy, Katina is going to Cumberland. I know you know she is going but you didn't know Ronnie got his daddy's car and they are going to be driving up there together in the car."

Then I heard her say, "Oh, oh, okay, wait a minute."

She called me to the phone and said, "Your daddy wants to talk to you."

I got on the phone, and he said to me, "I hope you have a real good trip and be a good girl."

"Daddy," I said.

"I know, I know," he went on, "but you know how your mother is."

I couldn't help but laugh a little. "But you did tell her it was okay for me to go?"

"Of course I told her," he assured me. "I like Ronnie a lot. He has been over to see me two or three times on his own, and we sat around until late at night sharing beers and talking. He's a good guy."

Ronnie hadn't told me about that part. I had expected the worst when I went to introduce Ronnie to my father. He never had liked any of the boys I hung out with in high school. And my mother—first, it was her idea for me to go visit Ronnie's family, and then she didn't want us to go when Ronnie showed up with a car. I was a bit overcome by the hilarity of it all.

We ended up having quite a trip to Maryland together. The journey took a lot longer than we had anticipated on account of a snowstorm. Driving through the mountains in the snow was a new experience for me, and it nearly scared me to death a few times when we were going around curves and slipped on the ice some.

We arrived late at night, going down a little alley behind the Harper's home and entering through the back door, as Ronnie's folks ran a little neighborhood grocery store out of the front room of their home. We came into the kitchen and there were all these pies and cakes laid out on the kitchen table. His mother had been busy preparing for my arrival. She had done some painting, scrubbed and waxed the floor, cleaned up everywhere. Ronnie kept saying, "Boy, she sure got ready for you to come."

Ronnie's brother Dick was all dressed up and sound asleep on the couch. We woke him and he got their mother up. Dolly, Ronnie's mother, came down and fixed us coffee and prepared something for us to eat. We were starved by then.

Ronnie's father was out, working the nightshift on the railroad. I met him the next day and was a bit taken back when I first saw him. We were sitting around in the kitchen that morning when I heard Ronnie's mother say, "Here comes Myrl." She added for my sake, "Ronnie's dad."

I turned around and this black man walked in.

Those were the days of coal burning, steam locomotives, and Ronnie's dad loved the railroad. His face and hands were black with coal dust. He was literally covered. He had been shoveling coal into a steam engine all night.

When he took his railroader's hat off, he was all white from the hat line up.

Ronnie's mother looked at me and said, "Looks awful, doesn't he? He's not going to touch you because the first thing he has got to do is go in and take a bath."

He looked at me with a twinkle in his eyes. "Fooled ya, didn't I? Must have scared you there for a bit?"

"Well, I don't know," is all I could say.

From then on I could always detect a bit of playfulness in his look, like the devil prancing in his eyes.

It didn't take me long to win him over. I thought he was such a nice man. A very gentle, precious person.

After he had his bath and some breakfast, we were all sitting around the dining room talking. I started saying something to him, then paused and asked, "Do you mind if I come over and sit on your lap?"

I didn't even consider what Ronnie's mother would think.

And Myrl said, "Sure Honey, come on over here and have a seat."

I went over and took a seat on his lap, then asked, "Well, do you mind if I give you a hug? If I'm going to sit here, I have to give you a hug."

"Oh sure, I'd love to have a hug," he replied.

I didn't realize until afterward what an unusual exchange that was for anyone in Ronnie's family. Ronnie told me they just didn't touch one another. Hugging and kissing wasn't something they usually did. This was a big difference between our two families. I was raised to hug and kiss whenever I met members of the family or felt like it. I always did like that part of my family upbringing. I had to warn Ronnie and his family that when they met my family, they had better be prepared. "You are going to have to get used to it, because you are going to get hugged by my daddy, my mother and everyone else in the family."

Nonetheless, I really liked Ronnie's family, all of them. To me it was more evidence that our relationship was meant to be.

Over the next couple of days I began to understand more why all the elaborate preparations had been made for my arrival. Ronnie's twelve-year-old sister, Joyce, started asking me questions at one point. She wanted to know, "Do you live in a white house with white pillars in the front?"

"Well, yeah," I answered.

We did. It was a small white house with a little porch out front.

But she wanted to know more. "Are the pillars round?"

"Yeah," I replied, "the house has a porch with a guardrail around it and pillars holding up the roof."

What I didn't realize was that she was thinking "Gone with the Wind." She was just so impressed.

Ronnie's parents had come to the conclusion there were only two classes in the South—and North Carolina was really in the deep

South. There were the rich people who owned the large plantations and there were all the other people who worked on those plantations. His parents had faith in their son and figured he wouldn't pick anybody who was poor. That left only one alternative. I had to be from a very wealthy family.

Later I overheard Ronnie's dad asking him if giving me $10 for Christmas would be enough. That may not sound like much now, but I was making $14 a week working as a teller for the Bank of Charlotte at the time. I thought, "God almighty!"

And I told Ronnie, "I don't need that kind of money."

"You'll hurt his feelings if you don't take it," was Ronnie's reply. "Just accept it and save it toward our wedding expenses."

Which I did, but it just seemed there wasn't enough they could do for us.

We stayed there for Christmas but had to leave the next day to get back to our respective responsibilities in North Carolina. Not having the car to go home with, Ronnie accompanied me on the train as far as Washington, D.C. Ronnie's dad was able to get free passes on the train for us.

Ronnie needed to catch his connecting train immediately when we arrived, and I had a three-hour layover. We said our goodbyes and Ronnie walked off, leaving me to look for a seat in a large, busy train station with a lot of strange men around.

I had never been anywhere like that alone before. I was still looking for a seat when I heard Ronnie call to me. He had had a change of mind. He didn't want me to have to be there unaccompanied among strangers for three hours. So he decided he would skip catching his train, stay to see me off, then thumb his way down to Camp Lejeune. I was most grateful. I just knew I had found a man who really cared for me.

St. Patrick's Catholic Church (now a cathedral) in Charlotte, where we were married in 1952. *(courtesy of B & H Photo Co., Charlotte, N.C.).*

Chapter Twelve

OUR WEDDING

It started out to be a small wedding, but Daddy insisted it be a big wedding.

"Daddy," I told him, "you can't afford a big wedding and neither can I."

We ended up having a pretty big wedding, with more guests than we knew what to do with. The whole event turned into a comedy of screw-ups and misunderstandings.

I wanted to get married on Valentine's Day, the 14th of February. Daddy couldn't take the weekend off from working at the restaurant. So we were married on the 12th, a Wednesday. Ronnie was discharged from the Marines the week before and I had just quit my job at the Bank of Charlotte.

We planned a Greek party for the night before at our home in Charlotte. My brother George arrived early from Florida ready to rock and roll. He rolled up the rug on the living room hardwood floor and pushed the dinning room table back in preparation for some energetic dancing. He also immediately took a liking to Ronnie.

Guest began arriving. We never could talk Ronnie's father into coming. "He doesn't do weddings and funerals," is the reason Ronnie's mother gave. She came with a sister of hers named Lena. Her other sister, Nellie, got mad when she heard Lena was coming and decided she wasn't going to come.

But there were plenty of others who showed up from out of town. My Aunt Edna accommodated some of them in her apartment just up the

KATHERINE HODGES AND RONALD LEE HARPER
are shown selecting their wedding china.

To Wed R. L. Harper

MISS HODGES GIVES HER WEDDING PLANS

Invitations have been issued which read as follows:

"Mr. and Mrs. James George Hodges request the honour of your presence at the marriage of their daughter, Katherine Tessie, to Mr. Ronald Lee Harper on Tuesday, the twelfth of February, at six o'clock in the evening, Saint Patrick's Catholic Church, Charlotte, North Carolina."

Plans have been completed and are announced today for the marriage of Miss Hodges and Mr. Harper, who is the son of Mr. and Mrs. Myrl L. Harper of Cumberland, Md.

The Rt. Rev. John P. Manley will officiate at the double ring ceremony, and the nuptial music will be presented by Mrs. H. D. Kendall, organist, and Charles Coira, vocalist.

The bride will be given in marriage by her father, and the bridegroom's father will be best man.

Ushers will include Pfc. Alfred J. Hodges of Wilmington, brother of the bride, and Richard Harper of Cumberland, Md., brother of the bridegroom.

Mrs. Robert W. Foster will be the bride's matron of honor, and the bridesmaids will be Miss Kathleen O'Connor and Mrs. William Walker, all of Charlotte.

Carol Ann Wally, daughter of Mr. and Mrs. C. H. Wally of Charlotte, will be flower girl, and Larry Gettier, son of Mr. and Mrs. G. L. Gettier, will be ringbearer.

Honorary attendants will be Miss Nancy Brigman, Miss Mary Beatty, James Stallings and Roger Cleaver.

Following the ceremony, the bride's parents will entertain at a reception at their home on Kenilworth Ave. Assisting will be Mrs. Edna Schneidt, Mrs. Elsie Moser and Mrs. J. M. O'Connor.

Mrs. Schneidt, aunt of the bride-elect, entertained at a linen shower at her home on Kenilworth Ave. Jan. 14. Thirty-eight guests attended.

Mrs. C. H. Wally and Mrs. Helen N. Allison will entertain at the former's home on Lumina Ave. Wednesday at a kitchen shower in honor of Miss Hodges.

Following the wedding rehearsal. Miss Hodges and Mr. Harper will give a buffet supper party in honor of their attendants at the former's home.

Selecting wedding china,
February 1952.

street from where we lived. Others we put in available rooms in our home. No one thought about where I was going to be spending the night before my wedding when Ronnie's mother and aunt were put in my room.

Many friends came by for the party the night before. George had invited all of his friends. Daddy must have invited half the Greek community in town. I, of course, wanted my friends there. Things became pretty lively.

Once the dancing started I really got caught up jitterbugging with George. Dancing is something I've always loved, ever since Daddy used to let me stand on his shoes to learn the steps when I was a little girl, and he'd lift me up and swing me around. George was a superb dancer and so much fun. He was into picking me up and twirling me around. I just loved it. Just about everyone who wasn't dancing was stomping the floor and clapping to the music.

About an hour into the festivities, Ronnie's mother came over to me and said, "Katherine, you need to go check on Ron."

I looked around the room and said, "Where is he?"

"I don't know," she said, "but if he is anything like his daddy, he is back in some room pouting."

This was the night before we were to be married.

I went looking for him and found him in a bedroom lying on top of the covers with his clothes on. He was feeling a bit left out, with me getting all carried away dancing with my brother.

I'd been warned that in his family people didn't get so physical. And it took some cajoling to get him to come out and try to let loose a bit on the dance floor.

When the Greek food had all been consumed and the music finally ended, people started leaving. And when our friends were all gone and it was time to go to bed, I asked my mother, "Where am I going to sleep?"

She looked at me and said, "Oh my goodness, I don't know."

So I suggested I go over to Aunt Edna's. But Mother wouldn't hear of it. "Oh no, no, no. Ronnie is over there and you can't see him before the wedding. I guess you'll have to sleep on the couch."

"But Mother," I protested. "I'm the bride, for God's sake."

In the end, I spent the night on the couch.

The wedding was scheduled for 6:00 p.m. the next day. I wanted my friends at the Bank of Charlotte to attend, and they didn't get off work until five. A bunch of us went down to Mother's hairdresser in the morning, and then I surprised my friends at the bank by dropping by to make sure they were all going to be at the wedding.

Little did I know I would be the last to arrive at the church.

When I got back to our house and began to get myself ready, the activity around me became frenzied. Mother just acted like she was on another planet. I got the feeling she thought I—the bride—was unimportant.

Later she told me, "I was trying all the time to keep from crying because you were my baby and you were leaving, so I just had to stay away from you as much as I could to keep from bursting into tears."

I had concluded she was glad to be getting rid of me.

About then was when the photographer called to say he wasn't going to be able to make it. This was a young fellow I had gone to school with, Scotty Stallings.

"Good God, Scotty," I gasped. "We are getting ready to go to the church. Did you get someone else lined up to come?"

Well, he hadn't bothered. "You better not even come near me for at least a year," I screamed into the phone. "If I see you, I'll kill you."

The hairdresser and Aunt Elsie showed up around four thirty, when I was still running around in a slip trying to help everyone else out with their details. They cornered me and insisted I get my dress on.

My wedding gown was made for me by a lady who worked at Belk's as a seamstress. She introduced me to what was called "candlelight white." I didn't like stark white and fell in love with this darker shade. For my bridesmaids, I went with "candlelight colors": light blues and pinks, and light mint green.

There were a dozen of my friends who wanted to be bridesmaids. I told them I couldn't afford so many. But they said they would be willing to buy their own dresses. In the end I had three bridesmaids and ten honorary bridesmaids.

I had tried my dress on once at the final fitting, but getting into it made me so nervous I couldn't do my makeup. The hairdresser stepped in to help.

She kept saying to me, "Don't you cry. Don't you cry."

By the time I was ready, most everyone else had left for the church. Alfred's wife, Janet, was my matron of honor. I saw her standing near the door with something in her hand.

"Janet, what is that in your hand?" I asked.

"Oh, my gosh," she said, like she had lost track of what she was holding. "These are Ronnie's suspenders for his tux."

"What are you going to do with them?" I inquired, beginning to imagine Ronnie's pants slipping down just as he was reciting the wedding vows.

"Well," she said, "I was supposed to give them to Alfred to take to Ronnie."

Alfred, the one who had done the matchmaking, was the best man in the wedding.

Janet flew out the door, looking for someone who could deliver the suspenders to Ron.

By then everyone else had cleared out and headed over to the church. My brother George was supposed to come back with the car to pick me up. There were just two of us, Janet and me, left at the house.

We stepped outside to wait. It was a beautiful February evening, unseasonably warm, though overcast. And we waited, and waited, and waited. The wedding was scheduled for six and it was ten minutes 'til.

Finally I saw a neighbor driving by. He looked over at us and promptly pulled in the driveway with a puzzled look on his face.

"What are you doing here?" he asked.

"Waiting for somebody to pick us up," was my response.

"Oh my God, get in the car. I'll take you," he said.

As we were driving over to the church he related to us, "Something just told me to check and make sure everyone had a ride. That was the only reason I went back around the block. But I didn't expect to find the bride stranded."

We made it to the church by six o'clock. I hiked up my dress and started running up the steps to the front door of the church. Monsignor Manley was standing just inside the door.

God bless his heart. He said, "Just slow down. We can't have a wedding without the bride."

I needed to hear that. A light drizzle had just started coming down. "It is a sign of good fortune," the monsignor said.

His calm reassurance was almost undone by my mother's hysteria. She came running over when she saw me, demanding to know where the marriage license was.

I could only say, "But I don't have it. I gave it to Alfred. He's the best man."

"Well, he doesn't have it," she stammered. "You can't get married without the marriage license."

I started crying.

The monsignor spoke up, "I know you had the marriage license. We can go on with the ceremony. We'll find the license."

He walked over to one of the ushers and informed him it was time to seat the mothers. My mother was a nervous wreck by then. She really was.

The monsignor knew the hairdresser and he approached her and said, "I hope you brought some patch-up, because the bride's mother just went over and jumped all over her, and got her crying."

I appreciated that. By the time I was patched up the bridesmaids had filed in, and Daddy was there at my side ready to escort me down the aisle.

We stepped into the sanctuary and paused briefly. I wish I could have tarried longer and enjoyed the atmosphere. The place was all candlelit, with candelabras down both sides and down the aisle in the middle. It really was a candlelight wedding.

Daddy started down the aisle with me on his arm. He wanted to just walk. We were supposed to take a step and stop, then take another step and pause. But Daddy couldn't do it. He suggested we dance down the aisle. I started laughing.

MRS. RONALD LEE HARPER, before her marriage Tuesday night in St. Patrick's Catholic Church, was Miss Katherine Hodges, daughter of Mr. and Mrs. James G. Hodges of Charlotte. Mr. Harper is the son of Mr. and Mrs. Myrl L. Harper of Cumberland, Md. Monsignor John P. Manley officiated. (Photo by St. John Studio)

Katherine in her wedding gown,
February 12, 1952.

When we arrived where George was sitting next to the aisle, he muttered, "Good God. It took you long enough to get here."

That really got me giggling.

Then I felt my garter drop to my ankle, and I thought, "Oh my gosh, what if it falls off my ankle and gets left in the middle of the aisle?"

I was preoccupied with my garter when we arrived at the front of the church and Daddy handed me off to Ronnie.

The ceremony was held outside the railing surrounding the altar. Ronnie wasn't a Catholic, so we couldn't be married up by the altar. I felt like I was being punished for marrying a non-Catholic, but the monsignor had told us it was a rule we'd have to abide by.

The ceremony progressed from there and I don't remember much about it. Someone had a little pocket Kodak camera. His miniature photos are all we have of the event.

Afterward George pulled his car up to the front of the church. Ron and I hurried down the steps and jumped into the car. Friends had wrapped it in toilet paper and streamers, and painted "Just Married" all over the windows. George took off with the horn blaring through the center of town, the long way home. When we pulled up to our house, where the reception was, we saw the red, flashing lights of a police car right behind us.

George told us not to worry. "Just get on in the house. I'll take care of it."

George was a policeman himself and managed to talk his way out of a "disturbing the peace" citation.

The fun at the reception was going well when, around eight o'clock, I looked around and couldn't see any of the groomsmen or bridesmaids. I couldn't imagine them leaving early, but at the same time, Ron and I did want to get out of there by eight thirty to head over to the room Daddy had booked for us at the Hotel Charlotte, the best hotel in town back then.

Still, people prevailed on us and the party went on. We didn't leave until close to midnight. We arrived at the hotel and checked in. A bellman accompanied us upstairs to our room. Just as he was putting the key in the door, he said, "I have to apologize. We didn't get to thoroughly clean the room before you got here."

I looked at him and said, "What? I don't want a dirty room."

Right then he threw open the door and a cheer went up from inside the room. What a scene! There were streamers strung from the ceiling fan to all corners of the room. The place was all messed up. All the bridesmaids and groomsmen, and a few others, had been drinking and having a ball while they awaited our arrival.

All I could say was, "Get out, get out, get out."

They were all laughing and feeling no pain, but they did file out.

All the windows were open and the heat had been turned off. The light bulbs were all missing, except in one small lamp. The shower curtain in the bathroom was gone.

What's more, the room had twin beds. This was our wedding night, and Daddy thought getting twin beds would make for a good joke.

We noticed something else funny about the beds. They weren't made up right. So I pulled the bedspread back on one and found the revelers had short-sheeted the bed and filled it with cracker crumbs and cigarette tobacco. They had done the same to the other bed as well.

It was past one o'clock before we finally got to bed. Then the phone rang. My brother George wanted to know, "Y'all wore the carpet out between the beds yet?"

I hung up on him, feeling angry. Then the phone rang again. It was Alfred this time. "Sis," he said, "We have to leave early in the morning so we are going to come down and have breakfast with you and Ronnie."

"What?" I replied. "Alfred, it's one in the morning." But he insisted on seeing us at 7:00 a.m.

We were down for breakfast at seven, and Alfred and Janet showed up.

As soon as they left I went straight to the front desk and said, "We do not want that room anymore. I want another room, with a double bed, and I don't want anyone to know what room we have. You tell no one what room we are in."

They agreed, then handed me a message. It was from Mother, saying we should come back to the house for dinner, since Ronnie's mother and aunt were leaving and we should see them off. Plus, she added, "You forgot your galoshes."

I could only say to Ronnie, "This is crazy."

"Sure is," he agreed.

We both really wanted to drop out of sight. Yet Ronnie was good-natured about it. We were planning to leave for Cumberland, Maryland, the next morning.

George came to pick us up to take us over to the house for dinner. He couldn't help but tease us some more.

"Having fun, aren't you?"

I was just looking forward to being on our way to Cumberland. Ronnie's folks had promised to let us use their car and pay for a honeymoon for us. We weren't sure yet where we were going to go, but I was imagining some peace and quiet away from everyone.

Chapter Thirteen

EARLY MARRIED LIFE

*T*he train ride up to Maryland two days after our wedding was crowded and uncomfortable. I kept visualizing being in Ronnie's parent's car and driving away on our honeymoon. When we finally did pull into Cumberland there was fresh snow on the ground. My mother was right; it was a good thing she had reminded me to take my galoshes.

Ronnie's mother met us at the door when we arrived at their home. Her first words were, "Oh Ronnie, Katherine, I'm so sorry. Dick (Ronnie's brother) took the car out last night and something happened in all the snow and ice, and the car was wrecked."

There went our plans for a honeymoon.

I looked at Ronnie and asked, "What are we going to do now?" figuring we would have to get a room in a hotel.

But Ronnie said we would have to stay at his parent's house. We couldn't afford hotel expenses. I knew there were three bedrooms upstairs in the house, but we weren't offered one. Rather, the foldout couch in the living room was made available to us.

And so for the first few weeks of our married life we slept on the couch in a busy household. Dick worked second shift and would come in late, traipsing through the living room on his way upstairs. Ronnie's dad worked whenever he was called and could be expected to parade through the living room at any hour of the night. Ronnie's little sister liked to come down and climb in bed with us early in the morning. Everyone was into making little teasing comments as they passed through. Needless to say, Ronnie and I weren't getting a chance for much intimacy.

Married life wasn't exactly getting off to a great start. Then I came down with a cold, and I overheard Ronnie's mother saying, "Oh, she is just homesick."

I wanted to cut and run right then and there.

It was a week or more before Ronnie found a job. His dad had a friend who gave Ronnie a job in a used-car lot. Ronnie's main responsibility was sweeping the snow and ice off the cars and washing them down every day, then starting all the cars up. He was paid twenty-five dollars a week and felt like he was overpaid for the little bit of actual work he did. He hated it and I didn't blame him.

I was eager to find a place of our own to live, a little apartment or something,—anything besides a living room couch in a busy household. Ronnie didn't think we had enough money coming in for an apartment.

"Then I'll find a job," I said.

And I did. Thinking the banks might not hire me, given how young I was, I went to the Montgomery Ward department store and gave them my background. They promptly hired me as a PBX operator, inserting phone lines into designated plug-ins to connect phone calls.

I was tickled to death and went home and told Ronnie, "Now we can get a place."

He was as delighted as I was.

After looking around a bit we found a little attic apartment in a house, with a separate entrance. The apartment had a good-sized kitchen/dining/living room area and a small bedroom and bathroom. We began settling into married life on our own.

Shortly thereafter Ronnie's brother Dick helped him get a job at a bakery on the swing shift. Ronnie would come home with his shirt all brown with baking grease from handling bread dough all day. We didn't have a washer and I took responsibility for washing his shirts, doing it by hand. It was real manual labor.

One day I had just bleached and washed all his shirts and underwear, and hung them all out to dry in the backyard. I was back up in our

apartment when I heard the landlady, who lived in the home downstairs, calling out to me. "Katherine, come quick, hurry. Did you hang some clothes outside? Hurry! Come now!"

I ran downstairs, only to have her say to me, "Oh, it's too late."

"What's the matter?" I asked.

"The train just passed," she said, "There are times of day when you don't hang clothes out."

We weren't far from the railroad yards and the trains passed just behind where we lived, billowing out black clouds of smoke from their coal-burning engines.

I went out to find the shirts I had just washed all black with coal dust. I pulled them off the line and sat down and cried.

Our kind landlady came out and said to me, "Honey, I am so sorry. I can tell you are not used to this."

"Well, I'm used to washing; I'm just not used to having to wash them all over again."

She took me into her home where she had a little washing machine and said, "I'll soak them and wash them, then you can hang them out when I tell you it is safe."

We got through that one.

I had a lot to learn about cooking as well. Daddy had always brought food home from the restaurant when I was growing up, and when we did have a big dinner at home, he would prepare the food. I knew how to do housecleaning, but I never learned much about cooking.

When Ronnie requested a chicken dinner, I went and bought what was available, a whole chicken. I took it back to our apartment eager to do a good job, but I had no idea what I was supposed to do with the chicken. I had never been taught how to cut up a whole chicken.

I called the lady downstairs, and she came up and showed me methodically how to cut up a chicken.

Then she asked me, "What are you going to do, bake it or fry it?"

I looked at her and asked, "Which is easiest?"

"Baking it would be a lot easier than frying it," she said, "since obviously, you have never fried a chicken before."

We had our baked chicken. But there was more to learn.

Watching Ronnie's mother cook and knowing how much he liked milk gravy, I tried making gravy for the first time. I thought I had it all figured out, having paid close attention when Ronnie's mother made it. But the first time I tried it on my own, it thickened up so much it was inedible, and I hid the result under the kitchen sink.

A few days later we had this horrible odor. Ronnie went looking for the source and found my gravy experiment under the sink.

"Oh my God, what is this?" he wanted to know.

I had to go back to his mother to ask what I was doing wrong. I had added hot water to it. His mother told me you had to use cold water. That made a huge difference in the outcome.

Slowly, I was catching on.

Back when we were preparing for our wedding and laying out our plans for the future, Ronnie was getting ready to be discharged from the Marines. He was nineteen, and in two years on active duty had moved up to the rank of sergeant. And, he had never gone to Marine boot camp. People find it hard to believe, but with the rush to prepare Marines for the Korean War, Ronnie was exempted from boot camp based on his performance in the reserves and on a written exam. Still, the Marines tried to get him to sign up for three more years, promising to send him to officer's training and offering him the rank of first lieutenant upon completion.

I told him he should do it if he really wanted to be an officer. But he wasn't so sure he did. Moving to Cumberland seemed to him the logical alternative, as he knew people there who could help him find employment.

However, things didn't work out well in Cumberland. Plenty of servicemen were returning from Korea and reassuming the jobs they had held before in places like the Celanese chemical plant and other industrial centers. Other job prospects were not promising.

I was doing okay at my job at Montgomery Ward, though the other young women working there resented me for having married one of the few attractive young men in Cumberland.

Then one evening our landlady yelled up from the bottom of the steps leading up to our apartment, saying, "Katherine, there is a policeman down here asking for you. It is something about your mother or dad."

That really scared me.

I ran downstairs. The policeman greeted me and said, "I don't mean to scare you, but your parents are worried and they want you to call them."

Mother always thought that when I got quiet and didn't communicate, something must be wrong. And I had totally neglected to stay in touch or provide my parents with a phone number where they could reach us.

"You need to call home right away," the policeman told me.

Ronnie was at work and didn't get off until late. I called home and Mother answered the phone. I was in a panic, thinking something had to be wrong.

Mother answered the phone. She quickly assured me everything was all right. Daddy had moved back home to Charlotte and opened a restaurant on West Morehead Street, which he called the Lafayette Grill.

Daddy got on the phone and immediately started saying he had found a job for Ronnie in Charlotte. "Well, to start off, he'll be driving a bread truck, but it is real good hours and real good pay."

Ronnie wasn't home, but I told Daddy I'd run it by him and see what he thought.

That was a Wednesday evening, and I had started bowling with Ronnie's mother on Wednesday nights. She showed up to take me bowling and I didn't say a word about the phone call. But I was just dancing inside and bowled a great game.

She kept asking me, "Why are you so happy?"

"Well, things are sort of settling down now," I told her, "and I'm just so happy to be married to Ronnie."

She was real pleased to hear that.

When Ronnie arrived home at the end of the swing shift, I gave him the word. The first thing he said was, "Oh boy, this is really going to upset Mom and Dad. You didn't say anything to them, did you?"

Ronnie was game. As he put it, "There is nothing going on here as far as jobs are concerned. Well, let's go back to your home."

I wanted it to be his decision and asked him, "Are you sure?"

He was, as he could see there was no real future in Cumberland. We called Daddy that weekend and said we would be down the following weekend.

When we informed Ronnie's mother, she tried to act like the news didn't upset her any; but she went on and on about how Myrl would be upset and probably wouldn't speak to us for a long time. In the end Ronnie's brother Dick gave us a ride down to Charlotte in the family car. We packed everything we could in the vehicle and arranged to ship the rest of our stuff.

In the midst of the move I began to feel increasingly sick to my stomach. A visit to a doctor confirmed my suspicion. I was pregnant. Having a life of our own in our own little apartment probably had something to do with it.

Back in Charlotte we moved in with my parents. Ronnie started going to work driving a bread delivery truck, leaving before dawn and not getting back until after dark in the evenings. Once I started feeling better, I began helping out in Daddy's restaurant as a waitress, and a little later I picked up a job at the Federal Reserve.

Still, I intermittently experienced morning sickness. There was one day when I was feeling particularly bad, swollen and really miserable. We mostly ate what Daddy brought home from the restaurant. Mother got to wondering what we would be having for dinner, perhaps thinking a change in diet might help me. She wanted me to telephone Daddy and ask him what he was going to be bringing home.

Calling Daddy and asking him what he was bringing home was an unusual thing to do, but I went ahead and made the call, not expecting the response he gave me. He immediately became all upset and started cursing at me. I was dumbfounded.

The exchange upset me so much that I was reduced to bawling my eyes out.

Ronnie arrived home earlier than usual that evening and found me still crying. Of course he wanted to know what the problem was.

Mother spoke up, saying, "It was her daddy."

Ron just said, "Okay, that's it."

I wasn't sure what he meant, but he told me to go to bed and try to get some rest. Mother brought a wet washcloth in to put on my forehead and tried to make me comfortable.

A little later I heard Daddy come home. I got out of bed and went over to the door and opened it a crack so I could hear what was going on.

I heard Ronnie saying to Daddy, "I don't care if she is your daughter, she is my wife and don't you ever talk to her like that again or we will move out of here tomorrow. I don't know where we will go, but I am not going to have you upsetting her the way you did."

I quickly shut the door and climbed back in bed.

After a few minutes Daddy came in and apologized to me. "Katina, I'm sorry. That's just me; that's just your daddy."

Never before had I heard my daddy apologize to anyone.

"Okay, Daddy," I said.

When Ronnie came in I gave him a big long hug, and he put his arms around me and held me. I was so proud of him.

Later that evening I heard Daddy in the kitchen saying to Mother, "Well, I'll never have to worry about Katherine. If Ronnie will stand up to me, he'll stand up to anybody. I'll never have to worry with him taking care of her."

From then on Ronnie and Daddy had a new mutual respect for each other. They got along well with each other. I was so proud. I had never had anyone take up for me the way Ronnie did that night.

THE CHARLOTTE NEWS

DEC 1 - 1952

Harper Infant's Funeral Is Held

Graveside services for Ronald Lee Harper, infant son of Mr. and Mrs. R. L. Harper of 1624 Kenilworth Ave., were held today at 5 P. M. at Forest Lawn Cemetery.

Monsignor John P. Manley of St. Patrick's Catholic Church officiated.

Survivors include the parents; and the grandparents, Mr. and Mrs. James G. Hodges of Charlotte and Mr. and Mrs. Myrl L. Harper of Cumberland, Md.; and a number of aunts and uncles.

Chapter Fourteen

RONNIE, JR.

We stayed with my parents in their home until after the birth of our first child, a difficult time in our early married life. I went into labor and was taken immediately to the hospital. The attending physician was the good old family doctor who had brought me into the world, as well as my brother Alfred. I thought I was in good hands.

By the time I was in the hospital, I was in active labor, with contractions coming about two-and-a-half minutes apart. I overheard one of the nurses say the doctor wasn't through having dinner and wanted the labor process slowed down. A nurse came in shortly after and gave me a shot, which put me to sleep.

When I awoke, I was startled, because I couldn't feel any movement from the baby. I called the nurse, and she came in with a stethoscope and listened for the baby's heartbeat.

Suddenly, she blurted out, "Oh, my God. Call the doctor immediately. We've got to get this baby going."

Of course I wanted to know what was wrong. But the nurse tried to reassure me, saying, "Don't worry, Honey. It's going to be okay."

The doctor arrived and, with the nurses, managed to get me started in labor again. Then they knocked me out with another shot. I don't know how long I was out. But I could feel myself going down a tunnel, sliding away. And I could see a light way off in the distance. I had no idea where I was going and, feeling afraid, I felt myself struggling to wake up.

When I opened my eyes I could see a nun leaning over me, holding a cool cloth on my face.

She was saying, "Oh poor baby, I am so sorry."

I looked up and asked, "What do you mean, poor baby?"

She was surprised I was awake, but said to me, "Well, let me put it this way. We are grateful you are alive."

"But my baby is dead," I concluded.

"Yes," she replied and left to get Ron.

I had hemorrhaged and they had had to give me three blood transfusions. The doctor and nurses were relieved I had survived.

Ronnie and Mother came in.

Ronnie spoke softly, "Honey, I'm so sorry."

I wanted to know about the baby.

"We had a little boy," he said. "He is beautiful. But he was stillborn."

I wanted to see the baby, but the medical people didn't think it would be good for me to see him. Ronnie ended up making arrangements with a funeral home and he took photos for me to see later.

I spent seven days in the hospital recuperating.

We named the baby, as we had planned: Ronald Lee Harper, Jr. He was just shy of seven pounds.

Years later when I was seeing another doctor and discussing with him my medical history, I asked him how my first child could have become so entangled in the umbilical cord that he was strangled.

The doctor said, "I'll tell you how, but let me first ask you some questions. Were you active in labor when you went into the hospital?"

I explained that I had been.

And he wanted to know what happened.

I told him I had heard the nurse say, "We have to slow her down because the doctor has gone out to dinner."

"They gave you a shot then?" he asked me.

I said, "Yes."

He then told me, "When they slowed the baby down, he was still struggling. That is when they turn, and that is when he got in trouble."

The tragedy of little Ronnie Junior's death brought to a close the first chapter in our married life. But there was so much more to come.

Enjoying some leisure in Florida in 1959.

Chapter Fifteen

MOTHER OF FIVE

Raising children was the most challenging job I ever had. My doctor even advised me at one point to get a part-time job outside the home to give myself a break from childrearing. He told me a job would be the kind of meaningful diversion I needed to keep from having a nervous breakdown. And he was right.

By then we had four children—Danny, Jimmy, Margie and Chris—and had been living in Greenville, South Carolina, for over a year. Ronnie had gone to work for Charlotte Textile Engravers in Charlotte in 1952, starting out as a common laborer. But his eagerness to work and his aptitude for learning led to a quick succession of promotions. When his company opened a new manufacturing plant in Greenville in 1957, Ronnie, at age twenty-five, was selected to be the vice-president and general manager of the new operation.

We moved down to Greenville and had to rent a house for a year. It was a difficult time for me, my first extended time away from Charlotte, which has always seemed like home. Greenville felt like a strange environment. But I had made up my mind it was going to work out. There was plenty for me to do, with three little ones, and another one on the way. Nobody else was going to take care of those kids for me.

My one true friend that first year in Greenville was a woman named Jenny Adams, whose husband, Cannon, was the assistant manager at the same division Ronnie worked for. They had moved to Greenville with their four children at the same time we had and lived in the same neighborhood. She helped me through some tough times.

Ronnie worked sixteen hours a day. He would be out the door on his way to work at six in the morning and often wasn't home until ten or eleven at night, just in time to have a bite to eat and go to bed, so he could get up early the next morning. Many times he didn't see the children until the weekend, and even on weekends he would often work. I knew he wanted to succeed and he had the necessary drive, so I did what I could to support him, knowing he was working for our benefit.

I did my best to keep the kids fed, changed and happy. That was a full-time job. In the evenings I would feed them a meal and put aside some of the dinner for Ronnie. I used to try to get the kids in bed by seven o'clock, using shades on their windows if it was still light outside. Once they were tucked away in their beds, I would set about doing the dishwashing and housecleaning until Ronnie came home from work.

I did find pleasure in the childrearing tasks. Most of all I just loved watching them grow and learn to do new things, and seeing their different personalities start to emerge. I think I tried to be more "old country" in raising my kids, doing things I had learned from my mother and grandmother. I thought they had some beautiful ways. For instance, in bathing a baby, I would wrap the child up in towels, papoose fashion, and add towels to the bottom of the little baby tub and build a little pillow. Then I would just bathe one section of their bodies at a time, so they were never fully exposed. After bathing them, I took olive oil and rubbed and massaged them all over and let them fall asleep in warm towels.

I know Dr. Spock's books were the general childrearing manuals of the day. Someone once gave me one of his books. I found his ideas confusing and stuck as much as I could with the old country ways I'd learned from my elders. I never beat my kids. I'd learned from my father how counterproductive that can be. But I would give them a smack on the fanny when they needed it. Most of the time they were so frightened by the time I got around to doing it that I didn't have to hit them hard to get the message across.

But life as a parent did get overwhelming for me at times. When I was about six months pregnant with Chris, I had some severe hemorrhoid problems. One week when Ronnie was going to be in New York attending

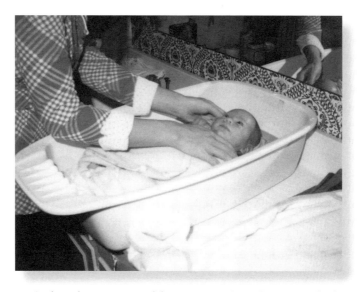

I tried to be more "old country" in raising my kids, doing things I had learned from my mother and grandmother, including taking special care in bathing them. This is me bathing our grandson Lee in 1975.

a seminar, I asked my mother to come down from Charlotte to help out with the children while I tried to recover. She was only with us for four days before Daddy drove down to get her early one morning.

"Get your clothes, Margaret," he said. "You're going home."

Being in pain, I was still in bed. Mother started crying.

"Go ahead, leave," I told her, not knowing how I was going to manage.

I called my friend Jenny. When she came over and saw me she said, "Katherine, I am taking you to the doctor."

"What about the kids?" I wanted to know.

Her four children were a little older than mine. She told me she would put her kids with mine and, "They will be okay. Under the threat of death, they are going to behave themselves until I get back."

I called my doctor and arranged to see him at his office. After examining me, he said, "I'm not sending you home. I'm sending you straight to the hospital. Your hemorrhoids are so bad, in and out, that I have got to get you into the hospital."

I didn't know what I would do. Ron was still out of town.

The surgeon refused to proceed with surgery until Ronnie was present. At first we weren't sure how to get in touch with him, but Jenny's husband finally got through, and Ronnie flew down from New York. I had my surgery and spent seven days in the hospital recovering. In the meantime, Ronnie transferred our three children to Charlotte so my mother could care for them there.

When I was released from the hospital, I was under strict orders to do nothing but sitz baths twice a day and rest. That only lasted a few days before I received a phone call from my mother saying that four-year-old Danny hadn't been feeling well. When she took him to a doctor, he was diagnosed with a heart murmur, and they were putting him in the hospital.

I immediately called my doctor and told him I had to go to Charlotte and explained why.

"You can't drive," he said. "You have to fly, and then only if someone picks you up at the airport and takes good care of you."

I arrived in Charlotte and went straight to Mercy Hospital. When I got to the admissions desk, I was told it was after visiting hours. The woman said she was sorry, but "You'll have to come back this evening."

"I'm not leaving here until I see my child," I insisted and started walking toward the elevators.

The woman at the admissions desk started yelling at me.

Just then a nun came down the hall. I happened to know her from high school. "Katherine," she exclaimed, "what are you doing here?"

When I told her my situation, she said, "Come along, child. Let's go." We went up and found Danny sleeping in a crib. I woke him up and he jumped up and hugged me, all overjoyed to see me.

I checked his chart and learned they were testing him for some kind of disease. Dissatisfied with the responses I was getting to my questions, I took him to my parents that afternoon. Ronnie arrived a few days later to take us all home.

I took Danny to our doctor in Greenville. He couldn't find anything wrong with him. But he did find fault with me, running around when I was supposed to be recovering from surgery.

"Well, you tell me who else can take care of my kids and I'll let them." I told him. "Ronnie can't stay out of work."

That was one real traumatic period for me. And there was more to come.

The stressors had been mounting for me for some time. I was experiencing recurring headaches. While all the above was happening, we were also building a new home. We purchased a lot in a new development and I worked with the salesman to help get the house designed to our specification. I learned a lot about housebuilding in the process. I had this idea of putting scenic wallpaper in the dining-kitchen area, with wood paneling below it. The builders had never done anything like it before and left it up to me to select what I wanted.

I was pregnant with Chris when all this was going on. About once a week I went by to check the progress on our new home. The house was close to being finished, with final coats of paint going on. The salesman called one day and said the scenic wallpaper had been put up and suggested I go by and have a look at the outcome of my idea. "It's

Our two older sons, Danny and Jimmy, during the time we were living on Lyndhurst Avenue in Charlotte, 1955.

beautiful. You'll love it. I know now why you wanted it because it really opened up that space," he told me.

I went over there to have a look and walked in the house. The salesman wasn't there. Then, all of a sudden, this guy comes out and starts screaming at me.

"What are you doing here? You're not supposed to be here. Get out of here."

All the workmen stopped what they were doing. They knew who I was.

"I beg your pardon," I said to him. "I'm soon to be the owner of this house."

"Well, you're not until the papers are signed," he shot back. "So you just leave now."

I was flabbergasted and looked around for the supervisor on the job.

"Who is he?" I asked.

"He's the builder, the one who owns the house until it is finished and sold," he told me.

By that point I was crying. "Why is he talking to me like that?" I wanted to know.

"Mrs. Harper," he said, "you need to go call your husband."

I went back home and, though I hated bothering Ronnie at work, I phoned him. He called the salesman for an explanation. The salesman got to the bottom of the issue. Some other person came in and looked at the house and liked what we had done, with the wood paneling and all, plus the scenic wallpaper. And he had offered the builder a higher price. The builder thought if he could get us upset enough, we just might back out of buying from him. The salesman urged us not to and to stick with the original, agreed-upon price. Ronnie had a stern conversation with the builder afterward, telling him he owed me an apology.

We did finally move into our new home. I think we paid $12,500 for it. Back then it was a pretty good price for a brand-new home.

My distressing encounter with the builder took some of the thrill out of moving into our new home. It was nice, but I was still homebound most of the time, looking after children.

Not long afterward Chris was due to be born and I went into labor. When I arrived at the hospital a nurse told me the doctor was going to be delayed and she was going to give me a shot.

Remembering vividly what had happened when I was in labor with little Ronnie, Jr., I refused, saying, "I don't want a shot."

The nurse suggested I go into the bathroom and empty my bladder. When I leaned over to flush the commode, I felt a prick in my rear.

I turned around and demanded to know, "Did you just give me a shot? I'll go to sleep."

They put me back in the bed and I felt myself going under. It was an awful, hot August day. The hospital was not air conditioned. I was a ball of sweat, just soaked through and through. I woke up ever so slightly and reached down to feel my uterus. Chris had been real active but now was moving very little.

I just started to scream, "Get the doctor now and start my labor. Start it back, now."

The nurses started scurrying around. They gave me another shot to restart the labor. Twenty minutes later Chris was born, healthy as can be. I was much relieved, but he added one more big responsibility to my already heavy workload.

On top of it all, not long after Chris was born in 1959, my father died. He developed a tumor, which turned out to be cancerous. Near the end Mother called, asking me to come up and visit him in the hospital. "Your daddy is looking for you," she said.

I made arrangements to have the kids cared for and headed to the hospital in Charlotte.

When I entered his room, Daddy was lying in bed with his eyes closed. My brother George was at his feet, while Alfred and Mother were on opposite sides of the bed. The scene remains vivid in my mind.

"Daddy, what are you doing?" I asked.

"Katina," he exclaimed, calling me by the endearing name he often used for me. "Come here."

I went to him and hugged him and kissed him. "Daddy, what's going on?" I wanted to know.

"Oh, I am really bad off," he acknowledged.

I tried to perk him up some. "You're going to do all right. You've got both of your boys here. I'm here. Mother is here."

But Daddy looked at me and asked, "Where's Ronnie?"

"He's on his way," I assured him.

"I'm not going anywhere until Ronnie gets here," he told me. "I've got to see Ronnie."

He absolutely loved Ronnie.

Shortly afterward Daddy was taken into surgery and suffered a heart attack while being operated on. We thought we lost him at that point. But they managed to stabilize him and get him breathing in an oxygen tent.

Ronnie arrived while he was still hanging on. That cheered Daddy up some. We both talked with him for awhile, telling him how much we loved him.

We left to go back to Greenville. Back in those days we didn't have cell phones, so we didn't find out until we arrived at our home in Greenville that Daddy passed away just shortly after we left the hospital.

I made it through the funeral, giving Mother the support she needed. But Daddy's death stirred up a lot of unsettled memories in me and added to my general unease. I was definitely reaching a breaking point.

I used to feel like I was in a different environment, stuck in the house with the children day in and day out. Sometimes when I did get out and meet with other couples, I'd find myself lapsing into "baby talk." I felt like I was getting to a place where I was going to lose my intelligence for functioning in the "real" world. I really did need some diversionary activity.

Fortunately, I had a good doctor, who recognized what was happening to me. He told me quite frankly one day, "You are on the verge of a nervous breakdown."

I looked at him and replied, "You can't be serious. What does a nervous breakdown feel like?"

He pointed out how I was letting things get to me and the head- aches I was having. Then he said, "I don't want to put you on any medication. But I want you to get away for two weeks, away from your kids."

All I could do was think of the four little ones I had at home. Danny was five; Jimmy was four, Margie was three; and Chris was just one year old. "I can't," I told him.

"Okay," he said, "I am going to give you a choice. You either go away for two weeks, ten days at least, or I am going to put you in the hospital. You need some rest."

I had a lot of faith in this doctor. This was in the old days when doctors used to actually listen to a person and take a real interest in each patient's well-being. Once little Chris woke up at three in the morning absolutely screaming and acting all agitated. I couldn't get him to settle down and stop crying and finally called the doctor at home.

"I'll be there in fifteen minutes," the doctor told me.

A bit taken aback, I asked, "It is the middle of the night, can't you just tell me?"

"Nope," he replied, "I have to see him."

The doctor diagnosed him as being severely dehydrated and sat with me for forty-five minutes while I spoon-fed Chris water.

I looked at the doctor and said, "What would I do without you?"

"Let me tell you something before you make me too big a hero," he responded. "I was getting ready to go fishing, and that is where I am going from here."

Nonetheless I thought a lot of my doctor and trusted him. I just didn't know how I could take two weeks off from childrearing responsibilities.

We had a neighbor living across the street who had grown up on a plantation owned by her parents in South Carolina. She was about seventy years old. She knew I needed help and I had told her what the doctor had said. She came to me one day and said, "Katherine, I believe I know somebody who could be of assistance to you, a woman who grew up with me on the plantation. She does housework and looks after children. I'm going to call her and see if she will come and help you out several days a week."

"Well," I said, "can you contact her?"

A bit later she called me to say the lady she had spoken of was going to be at my door early the next morning. "She'll take an early bus and she knows where I live because she has been here."

Ronnie had just left for work the next morning when Lillian, a spry, sixty-year-old African-American woman, showed up at the back door. Chris had managed to get out of his crib and was crawling down the hallway. When I opened the door, she said, "Hello, I'm Lillian. Oh, I got to get that baby."

She walked in, right past me, picked up Chris and started taking care of him. For me, she was like manna from heaven.

With Lillian coming two-and-a-half days a week to look after the children, I took my doctor's next suggestion and applied for a part-time position at the local bank. He told me I needed the diversion. As he put it, "I sense you are a talented person, and while it is important for you to be there for your children, two-and-a-half days a week of part-time work is not going to hurt your kids and it will do wonders for your well-being. Besides, it gives the kids a break as well and a chance to recognize someone else in authority."

The doctor was right. Being able to get out and work some, to be in an a position where I felt I could keep up with the times and not lose my adult mentality was important to me, and I think the kids benefited from my feeling more in touch with the world.

Not that I ever neglected my childrearing responsibilities. It was important to me to be there for the kids when they needed me. And it was always the agreement I had with whoever I worked for during the years our children were growing up: If something came up when I was at work, I wanted liberty to leave if my children needed me.

Life is very fragile. I used to worry more about something happening to me than Ron being incapacitated. What would Ron have done on his own with five children? My concern gave me an incentive to take care of myself, knowing how much others depended on me being healthy.

Having Lillian to help out made such a big difference in my life. She was a jewel, she really was. She lived in the projects in Greenville. Her husband wasn't worth salt. He was a "preacher" who never preached. I once suggested to Lillian that his being a preacher was his excuse for not working.

Lillian, who helped take care of our kids when we lived in Greenville. She made life so much better for all of us, 1958.

Her response was, "Honeychild, don't even go there." She said she "was out of the old, old school. Whether they are good or bad, you just don't turn them loose."

She had terrible arthritis and osteoporosis, with big knuckles and joints. But she didn't complain and was so willing to be helpful. I just loved her and so did the kids.

I would call home sometimes from work and Lillian would say things like, "I could have whipped them to pieces today."

I'd want to know what they did to get her upset.

"I put them down for their nap, got them all settled in," she explained, "With their Yogi Bear stuffed animals. Then I left the door cracked open so I could check on them later. When I did get back to look in on them, they were still in bed, so I went on doing the cleaning and all. Then I heard a little yell outside. When I checked, they were outside playing. They had put their stuffed animals in the bed and pulled the covers up over them to look like they were still in there sleeping. Oh, I could have whipped them to pieces today."

I could tell she loved it. She would end up sparing the rod, but on that occasion she did make them skip the treat she generally gave them in the afternoons.

She did so much more than just take care of the kids. She'd do the cleaning and dishwashing, and help get things ready for dinner. She didn't think I should have to do anything around the house. "You did your job," she'd say. "You had all your babies. You don't have to do anything else. I'll take care of it."

Lillian worked for us for the next few years, as long as we remained in Greenville, allowing me to continue with the part-time work I did at the bank. When our youngest child, Georgia, was born in 1961, with Lillian's help, I was able to work at the bank right up until two weeks before she was born. Then with my doctor's blessing, I was back at work four weeks after her birth. Lillian made life so much better for all of us.

Meanwhile Ronnie continued as the manager for the Charlotte Textile Engravers Greenville plant up until early 1962, when he finally got fed up with his supervisor and resigned. He tried a number of sales jobs afterward with limited success. So when he was offered a position with his old competitor at Consolidated Engravers in Charlotte, he was eager to get back to what he was good at doing. That is when he changed his name from "Ronnie" to Ron.

Leaving Lillian behind when we moved back to Charlotte was one of the hardest parts of the transition. I wanted her to come to Charlotte so badly, but it wasn't possible for her with her family in Greenville. I thought I had said my final farewell to her before we left. She had helped me pack everything up. I was sitting at the house waiting for the movers to come in the evening. At eight o'clock the doorbell rang, and when I opened it, there stood Lillian.

"I couldn't stand the thought of you here with those little babies and needing help, so I'm here for the rest of the day," she said.

We both started crying.

I did keep up with her after we moved to Charlotte. I couldn't believe it at first, but I learned that most of the people she had worked for in the past had not bothered to pay her Social Security. She was about sixty-three at the time, nearing the point when she could start collecting. I checked into the details and learned if I continued to pay her Social Security for a few more years, she would be eligible to draw benefits, so I did.

Three or four years later we made a trip down to Greenville and tried to look her up while we were there. She didn't have a phone number at that point, and I never did get the phone numbers of her two daughters. She was no longer living in the projects. Neighbors told us she had moved out, but they had no idea where she had gone. I grieved losing touch with her. She had made such a big difference in my life.

We sold much of our household stuff when we moved from Greenville back to Charlotte. We weren't able to sell our home in Greenville right away, but we did rent it to a captain at the airbase. In Charlotte we moved into a rented home for the first year. All we had was two chairs in the living room; our dinette table with six chairs; the bedroom sets for the kids, and Ron and I; plus our washer and dryer. The house, just off Eastway Boulevard, was smaller than what we had grown used to.

Within a year I said to Ron, "Let's start watching the paper."

"For what?" he wanted to know.

"For a bigger house. We need a bigger house."

"How are we going to afford that?" he asked.

"You don't worry about it. I'll work on it," I assured him.

I started watching the house ads in the paper and one day came across a classified reading, "House for sale by builder taking on trade. Builder will pay closing costs."

Intrigued, I called the builder and asked about the house. "Well," he said, "nobody has lived in it for a year and it is sort of a mess." But he told me it was on Windsor Avenue, right off Park Road and Poindexter Street, in what was known as the Sedgefield part of town, though people later took to referring to it as part of Dilworth to add prestige and value to homes in the area. It wasn't far from where I had grown up on Kenilworth Avenue.

Ron and I met the builder at the home the next weekend. Saying it was a bit of a mess was an understatement. The grass was a foot high in

Our home on Windsor Avenue in Charlotte, where we lived for thirteen years. I was pretty much a stay-at-home mom for much of that time, raising five kids of my own and keeping tabs on thirty-some other kids in the neighborhood, 1969.

the front and back yards. The toilets and the tub were black with mold. The floor in the kitchen was filthy. But we could see the potential. With the grass cut the yards would look great. The street was not a through street, making it a safe neighborhood for the kids to play in. School was a short walk away. The house could be cleaned up.

When we started talking price and the subject of the down payment came up, I suddenly realized I had forgotten all about that part, thinking "no closing costs" in the ad had meant there would be no up-front costs.

"Don't worry about it," the builder said. "You write me a check for the down payment and I will hold it until we close on the house. And then I am going to give it back to you."

I knew right then we had found the right house and the right person to be buying from. We paid $16,000 for the twenty-two hundred square foot home. Later when we managed to sell our home in Greenville, financing this new home in Charlotte was not a problem.

Our 50th wedding anniversary celebrated with a hundred friends on February 12, 2002. *(Photo courtesy of Joseph Martin)*

Our extended family of children and grandchildren, enjoying a Disney Cruise in 2002. *(Photo courtesy of Disney Cruises)*

Of course, I had to go to work with some Clorox and cleanser mixed together to get the place cleaned up. And the coal furnace that took up half the basement was always a bit of a hassle. Coal trucks would empty coal through a window into a bin in the basement. From the bin the coal had to be put in a feeder, which would automatically feed it into the furnace. Ron and the boys didn't care much for the chore of refilling the feeder, so most of the time I would go down and do the job rather than argue with them over it. We eventually converted to an oil furnace.

The neighborhood turned out to be a great place for raising kids. There were thirty-two children living in the area and they all played together in the street. I was pretty much the stay-at-home mom for many of the thirteen years we lived there, so if anyone got hurt, they would show up at our house. We knew everyone on the street.

For schooling I enrolled our three older ones in the Catholic school I had attended. For junior high they went to Sedgefield. And for high school they rode the bus up to Myers Park High School.

I liked having the kids wear the school uniforms that were required when they attended the Catholic school. It was a bit of an investment for us at first: five pairs of pants each, with five white cotton shirts. This was before there was wash-and-wear. And with Ron putting on a clean outfit every day, I was left with quite a laundry task. This was the early 1960s. There were no commercial laundry services. I did all the washing and ironing.

It was during our years living on Windsor Avenue that our children grew to be teenagers and fully developed their different personalities. I was forever intrigued by the process.

Danny, the oldest, was always an idealist and a good kid. I could always count on him to give me a truthful version of events. Not that he never got in trouble, though sometimes for things he didn't do.

His brother Jimmy came home from school one day saying Danny, in fifth grade at the time, had got in trouble.

"What did you get in trouble for?" I wanted to know, seeing a big red hand mark still on the side of his face.

Our oldest child, Danny, in
a grade school photo.

"Mom, I swear I didn't do anything," Danny told me, and I was inclined to believe him.

"Why did Sister slap you then?" his brother chimed in.

He had been standing in line in the cafeteria when some of the other fellows started a scuffle. What the nun saw was Danny laughing, and she concluded he was the chief culprit, then hauled off and slapped him.

That sort of behavior on the part of some of the nuns is something I did not abide. "Y'all stay in the house," I told the kids, and I got in the car and headed over to the school. The offending nun saw me coming when I entered the school and took off. I took off behind her, upstairs and down the hall. Failing to catch her, I dipped into the principal's office and told him what had happened. I let him know Sister was smart to get out of there when she saw me coming, because I was going to slap her across the face just like she had slapped my little boy.

The principal assured me she would apologize to me.

"No," I said. "I want her to apologize to Danny, because he did nothing wrong, and I think there is nothing worse than slapping a child for something he didn't do."

Incidents like that one, plus when we learned how many of the books in the school library were way out of date, and other things about the way the school was run finally led us to taking our kids out of the Catholic school. Ron and I actually did some fundraising to help update the school library collection, only to learn later that much of the money we raised was used to pave the church parking lot.

Danny, however, survived. He was a real sportsman and loved playing football, doing well on the high school team at Myers Park. He did have difficulty with authority figures telling him what he could and couldn't do sometimes, a response I thought was often justified. One of the coaches put a lot of pressure on him to be on the wrestling team when he didn't want to wrestle. One could understand why the coach wanted him. He was really into training and worked part-time in a gym, learning every muscle in the body and how to properly train. But he had no interest in being on the wrestling team, which led to conflict with the coach.

Danny also wanted to take some anatomy or biology class his sophomore year, eager to supplement what he was learning at the gym about body parts. He was told the class was only open to juniors and seniors. He was really into astronomy. We bought him a telescope and he learned the name of just about every constellation in the night sky. But when he wanted to join the astronomy class at school—again, he was told the class was only for upperclassmen. He tried to buck the system and I even went to bat for him, going and speaking with his counselor. In the mind of his counselor, Danny was just disobedient. "He doesn't want to abide by authority."

"Abiding by authority is not the issue," I protested. "We don't have problems with him at home. I want him to get into things he loves doing and wants to learn about, and you just want to make him wait. He's rebelling because he can't study what he is good at and wants to learn."

"Well," the counselor said, "if I had a child like that I'd just kick him out in the street and let him know what the real world is all about."

Danny dropped out of school shortly thereafter, at age seventeen. I continued to raise Cain at the school on his behalf, and the administration even changed some of their policies as a result, but it was too late for him.

He came home one evening and asked if he could take his dad and me out to dinner. We were surprised, but he was still working in a gym and had his own money. He took us out to the Driftwood Restaurant, a rather upscale place, and over dinner he told us, "I just wanted to let you know I joined the Marine Corps."

"What?" I exclaimed. "You are only seventeen."

"I'll be eighteen pretty soon, and if I can get you or Dad to sign for me, I can go in now."

I looked over at Ron, knowing what his response would be.

"We'll sign for you," he said.

Danny went in and was stationed at Parris Island, South Carolina. We went down for his graduation from boot camp. It was very impressive. His unit had put together a drill team that was just fantastic. Danny was one of the lead people on the field, and I thought he was just incredible.

Now, Jimmy was an altogether different character when he was growing up. Jimmy was an actor, on or off stage. We got him involved in a children's theater once when he was young and he played the back end of a donkey in one act. He got more applause than anybody else. What a character, even as the back end of a donkey! We just sat there and howled, it was so funny.

His humor, however, wasn't always so quaint and silly. When he was about seventeen he had a .22 rifle. I wasn't so happy about him having the gun, but he had it. One evening he wanted to go out with a friend and do some shooting. I told him, "Okay, but don't get yourself in trouble, because if you do and get thrown in jail, I'm not going to come down and get you."

"Oh, Mom," he said.

Ron was out of town, so when the phone rang about midnight, I was the one who answered it. A man's voice said, "This is Sheriff so-and-so and I have your son down here at the jail. We need to know if you'll come down and see us about him."

"Is he okay?" I asked.

"Yes ma'am, he seems fine."

"Good, just let him stay overnight and I'll come down in the morning," I told him.

Then I heard Jimmy in the background laughing and yelling out, "Mom, I can't believe you'd let me stay all night in jail."

What a character. He had put his friend up to making the call, wanting to find out if I'd really let him spend the night in jail.

He didn't let me forget it afterward. "You would have let me stay in jail, wouldn't you have?" he'd remind me.

"Yep," I'd answer. "That is the way I feel about it."

Joke or no joke, there were times Jimmy could be fiercely independent and display a fire-brand temper. He got the best of me once when he ran off and didn't come home for three days. This was when he was in about the eighth grade. I became so worried about him I contacted a minister. The minister told me to just put my son in God's hands.

"I've already done that," I said.

"He will come home," he assured me. "And when he comes home, I want you to run out to him like the father with the prodigal son and hug him and tell him you are so happy to see he is okay. I'll guarantee you he is going to be dirty, but I want you to bring him into the house and have

Jimmy, 1961.

him take a bath. Tell him while he is bathing you will fix him something really good to eat. Then feed him a delicious meal."

"I don't know if I can do all that," I replied.

"You are going to have to do it, because you want to show him you are grateful he is alive and well."

For three days I anxiously waited. Danny didn't know where Jimmy was. Margie didn't know. We did get word, however, from some of the other kids in the neighborhood that he was okay. "Don't worry about him," they told us.

After three days I was looking out the window when I saw him coming down the street, looking haggard. I ran out to greet him. He was filthy dirty, but I threw my arms around him and gave him a big hug. I was so relieved to see him and to know he was okay. I told him to go in and take a bath and I would fix him something to eat.

He took a long bath and then came out for the meal I had prepared. While eating he explained to me where he had been. He had spent three nights and days hidden in a culvert. His friends brought him food and whatever else he needed. I let him know he worried me a lot, but more than ever, I was so happy to see him back. He never told me why he did it, though he never did it again.

Our third child, Margie, was the one I could always depend on. She loved to help with the cooking and voluntarily did the dishes. Margie was more introverted and contemplative, a good kid to the point of wanting to keep others in line.

One day I saw her running across the street toward our house, and then swing around into the backyard. Next, this Greek lady who lived up the street came chasing after her. Apparently she couldn't find Margie in the backyard, so she came to the door. When I answered she starting talking in Greek a mile a minute.

"I'm sorry," I said. "I don't understand what you are saying."

She just kept jabbering in Greek, though I did gather she was looking for Margie.

She finally gave up and left, and I went out to the backyard to look for Margie.

Margie in grade school, 1964.

She was nowhere in sight, so I called out, "Margie, where are you? I know you are here someplace."

She came crawling out of the little entrance to the doghouse.

"How in the world did you get in there?" I wanted to know.

"It was easy, Mom. I didn't want her to catch me."

"Why was she chasing you?"

"Because I slapped her granddaughter, who had it coming."

I inquired further. "Okay, now is that really the way it happened?"

"Mom, honest to goodness. She was picking on someone else and I told her to stop and she wouldn't, so I finally told her 'If you don't stop I'm going to slap you.' I did and she went running to her grandma."

I let it go. It seemed justified. But I always was amused how Margie ended up, literally, in the doghouse for what she had done. I never forgot the sight of her crawling out through the little doorway.

Chris, our youngest son, was the only one of our children who, when he started walking, wanted to go outside. He started walking at about nine months. We were still living in Greenville, and he would always head for the door and want to go out. Most kids learn the word "no" early enough. Chris learned the word "outside" before he learned "no."

We had to build a little fence in the carport so he could play out there. He was the only one I had to buy a snowsuit for, because, even in the winter, he preferred to play outside. I would put his toys out in his fenced-in area and he would be happy as a jaybird. It didn't matter what the weather was, he wanted to be outside.

As he grew older he became good in sports. He took up speed skating on roller skates, back before there were in-line skates. He was good at it. In high school he played football and was a real star. I never understood the game very well, but we would all go to the home games when Chris was playing for Myers Park High. As soon as the game was over, we'd see him going off with his arm around a cheerleader. He was a popular guy.

He did have problems starting on projects and not carrying through and finishing them, or getting really into something and then quickly losing interest. We'd do our best to encourage him in whatever interests he had by buying what he needed to pursue his passions. He got hooked

Chris as a young man, popular, athletic and intelligent, 1975.

on music and wanted to learn to play the drums. We bought him a drum set and he lost interest soon after. Finally, when he was in junior high school, we insisted he get a paper route and earn enough money to pay for half of whatever he needed for his current passion, figuring he would be more likely to stick with it longer.

Popular, athletic and intelligent, Chris was also a loyal friend—to a fault. He used to give rides to school to some of his friends. A few of those friends were not the most upright characters, but Chris was into "rescuing" them, including those with growing drug habits. When the police stopped him once and searched his car, they came up with LSD hidden up under the dashboard. Chris was arrested.

We had to get an attorney involved to help with the matter. Chris, loyal friend that he is, would never tell which of his friends put the drugs in his car, though he insisted he knew nothing about the drugs being in the car before he was stopped. The case dragged on for almost a year. I hated seeing his name in the paper each time there was a hearing. At the close of the final hearing, the judge told Chris to "turn and face your parents and apologize to them for what you have put them through this past year." Then the judge gave him six months probation.

I was so relieved he only got probation and made sure he followed it. In the end I could admire him for his loyalty but insisted he be more careful in selecting his friends.

Georgia, our youngest, was a little princess. We see little girls on television in beauty contests, with tiaras on their heads and jewelry around their necks and wrists, with sprinkling stuff glittering up their costumes. That was where Georgia wanted to be. So much of the time she was lost in fantasy.

She was always real prissy, but also a free spirit. She wanted to take ballet lessons when she was young. All the practicing got to be too much for her. She liked to be more free-flowing, not choreographed. She wanted to do her own thing.

Georgia was fashion conscious from a young age. From the time she was in second grade, I could not buy her any clothes and bring them

Georgia as a young girl, already gregarious and outgoing, 1965.

home to her. She insisted on picking out her own outfits, otherwise she wouldn't wear them.

I always thought she would grow up to be an actress or a dancer. She was gregarious and outgoing. She laughed a lot.

Five kids was more than a handful for me at times. Still, I treasure the memories I have of raising them. More than any other house we lived in, our kids remember our home on Windsor Avenue as the home they grew up in. We have a lot of memories attached to that place.

When we finally sold the house, after building our present home, we got $32,500 for it. When I added up the costs of all the improvements we had made—installing an oil furnace, fixing up the basement, putting on a new roof and all—the total came to $16,000. So we didn't have to pay capital gains taxes when we sold the house.

Our accountant wanted to know how we had done it. Ron figured it was coincidence. When things like that happened, he would say, "Oh, it is just another coincidence."

I never believed in coincidences. Anything happening of that sort was never a coincidence for me.

Birthdates of Our Children

DANNY HARPER ∽ DECEMBER 17, 1953

JIMMY HARPER ∽ APRIL 10, 1955

MARGIE HARPER KLUTTZ ∽ JULY 28, 1956

CHRISTOPHER HARPER ∽ AUGUST 15, 1958

GEORGIA HARPER EHRENBERG ∽ MARCH 16, 1961

Too often, I think, women sell themselves short in evaluating marriage and childrearing. Ron and I were recently out to a fundraising event. We were seated at a table with three couples. Being always interested in what people do, we started asking the others about themselves and what they did. The men had ready answers, telling about their jobs and what their specialties were. Two out of the three women said, "I'm just a housewife."

I couldn't help but ask, "Do you have any children?"

One of the "just-a-housewife" women had three children and the other had two.

"No, then," I said, "You are not just a housewife. You manage what your husband brings home, and you manage your children's lives. You have a proper profession."

I told them I had been in their position, with five children. I did a lot of multi-tasking. I could virtually do five things at one time, being on top of all five kids and their five grades at school, being involved in PTA activities, keeping the family fed and the household functioning, staying informed about what Ron was doing at his workplace, not to mention taking care of myself. I was not "just a housewife." It was the toughest job I ever had.

I was just getting started on the topic, but one of the other husbands at the table piped up and said, "I think we ought to get off this subject."

As I Lay Me Down to Sleep
I Pray the Lord My Soul to Keep

Dearest Mom & Dad,

As newborns your Love brought us to life.
No differently than when God brought Adam up
    from the dust,
Breathing life and his Love into Adam's body and soul.
And from Adam's rib,
      God created his companion and soulmate, Eve.

Like God, Adam and Eve—you knew that each of us
As your children, would also face life-long temptations.
Yet you've always encouraged us to be strong when the tides
Turned away because of you own personal experiences.
Like God, you've continually praised us
      for our honesty and belief in a higher power.
And you've shown each of us the true meaning
      behind tough Love.
Like God, you've stood by our sides as we gave our Loving
Breath to your fourteen grandchildren
      and five great grandchildren.

The Lord, his Love, is Now our universe.
What we've thrown out to the universe you've always
Seemed to catch with grace and ease. Be it good or bad.
More importantly, at the end of the day, you've
ALWAYS treated us with respect.
Like God, you've treated us with dignity,
And have shown much pride in our work to achieve
Our personal goals. We thank you both for breathing life
Into our bodies and our souls. We thank you for being brave,
by volunteering to be our parents.
We thank you for being our teachers,
    quiet mentors and counselors.

As I lay me down to sleep, I pray the Lord my soul to keep.
When I awake to sunshine bright,
May I know that WE are filled with his Delight.

Love always and forever,
Your beloved children.

MERRY CHRISTMAS, 2006

Danny ~ Jimmy ~ Margie ~ Chris ~ Georgia

Chapter Sixteen

ON BEING "BLACK" IN CHARLOTTE

I think it was the summer 1947, between my ninth and tenth grades in high school, when I spent ten days at the beach. I would have been fourteen years old. I had a good friend whose mother and father invited me along on their vacation. Little did I know what ten days in the sun could do to a person.

My friend and I hit the beach at eight or nine every morning we were down there, lying in the sun until we were ready for lunch, soaking up the rays. We became real sun-worshipers. We would head in for lunch, followed by a nap, then be back on the sand by about three-thirty. Only when the sun was getting low in the sky and it was time for dinner, would we go back in. We followed the same routine every day for ten days and had a great time.

When we got back to Charlotte, the family I went with dropped me at my home in Kenilworth. With my hair all tied up in a bandana, I was feeling good to be home after a great vacation. I rang the doorbell and stood there waiting patiently, expecting my mother to open the door and welcome me home.

When the door finally opened, I heard my mother ask in a gruff voice, "What do you want?"

"Mother," I replied, "Why are you talking to me like that?"

"Katherine. Oh, my God. What did you do to yourself?" Mother blurted out.

"What? What are you talking about?" is all I could say.

She quickly opened the door, nearly knocking me down, saying, "Get in here. Your daddy is going to be furious. Look at you."

I still didn't know what she was talking about.

She grabbed my arm and exclaimed, "Look at your arm."

"Yeah," I said, "Isn't it pretty?"

I had the best tan I'd ever had in my entire life.

"Oh, it is a disgrace," was all mother could say for it. "Oh, it's going to be awful. You are absolutely going to get in trouble."

I defended myself saying, "All I did was get a good suntan, like everyone else at the beach."

"Yes," she said, "but with your olive skin you became darker than most people. You are going to have to do something. You can't go out of the house looking like that."

"Looking like what?" I wanted to know.

She just kept saying, "People are not going to speak to you. People are not going to know you. And they are going to be mean to you."

I had no clue what she was talking about.

Well, I didn't stay in the house. The next day I boarded a city bus to head downtown to my father's restaurant. When I got on, I went about halfway back in the bus and sat down, thinking nothing in particular. People around started staring at me. I was naïve enough to think people were actually admiring my tan. But nobody in that bus full of white folks sat next to me or even close to me.

By evening when I caught a bus to go home, I was beginning to grow a little more suspicious of other people's behavior. People seemed to be looking at me with hard, cold stares. Nobody sat next to me. When some black folks boarded the bus, even they gave me piercing looks as they passed to the back of the bus, where they were required by law to sit. The bus driver kept studying me in his rear-view mirror. The whole experience became a little too unsettling for me.

I ran home from the bus stop. "Mother," I cried, when I entered our home. "I don't understand it."

"It happened, didn't it?" she blurted out. "Nobody would sit next to you on the bus, would they? Did anyone say anything to you? Did you get put off the bus, or get told to move to the back?"

"No, but why would they?" I wanted to know.

"Because they think you are a Negro," she finally said. "The only thing that saved you was your facial features. They couldn't figure you out. I warned you."

The reaction from my school friends was different: "Wow, where did you get that tan?" Still, I was glad when my tan began to fade and go away.

More than anything else, my experience of being "black" for a short time taught me much about race relations in Charlotte in the years before the civil rights movement. Suddenly I became more conscious of all the signs over the drinking fountains and restroom entrances saying "whites only." I began to take note when I saw black people go to the back of the buses to find a seat. I became more aware that there were no black kids in the schools I attended.

I also began to appreciate more the subtle ways in which my father showed his disapproval of the segregation policies of the time. Perhaps it was because of his early life experiences of the discrimination between Turks and Greeks, and the prejudices he felt within the Greek community even in America. He did not go along with many of the prejudices often exhibited in the Greek-American community. "Greeks marry Greeks" was a frequent refrain—one he chose to ignore when he married my mother. Other Greeks used to accuse him of marrying a "white" woman. He hadn't known about "blacks" and "whites" growing up and the whole racial segregation system in place at the time just seemed unnatural to him.

Daddy was active in getting the Greek Orthodox Church started in Charlotte and he stayed active in AHEPA, the Greek civic organization, for many years, but he detested any overt Greek favoritism. I recall once when a Greek Orthodox priest was giving him a hard time for not having taught his children to speak Greek.

He made it clear, "I'm Greek as far as where I was born and raised. I'm American now that I am here. My children were born here and they are Americans."

That was end of it. We could understand why he called his first restaurant the Little American Restaurant.

He always showed respect for black folks, beginning long before the civil rights movement in the South. And though there were boundaries he couldn't cross in southern society at the time, like letting black folks mingle with white customers or work as waitresses, he did find other ways to accommodate them. He always kept a table in the kitchen where he welcomed his black customers. And he would let them use the restrooms when there weren't any white customers around.

The Presbyterian Church we sometimes attended would often call Daddy up if there was a homeless family needing to be fed. He never turned them away, no matter what the color of their skin. After my innocent experience being "black," these little acts of kindness without regard to race began to become more noticeable to me.

The civil rights movement swept through the South in the mid-1960s, during the period when our children were attending Myers Park High School. School integration became a priority and "busing" became one of the solutions. That is, many of the black students who had been attending sub-standard, segregated, all-black schools in impoverished neighborhoods were bused to previously all-white schools in other parts of the city. Myers Park High School was smack in the middle of one of the most affluent neighborhoods in town and received busloads of black students. The program did not always go smoothly.

Jimmy and Margie were in high school during the worst part. I remember hearing an announcement on the radio one day telling parents not to go to the school. This was before I knew what was happening. The announcement kept emphasizing, "Stay at home. The police have the situation under control."

I was about to go crazy, fearing the worst, yet waiting for my kids to get home from school. A race riot had broke out on campus. Margie said it was terrible. She blamed the principal for doing little to quell the disturbance, locking himself in his office and only appearing when he had an armed escort. The school was closed for several days, then steps were taken to bring the students back, one class at a time, while discussion groups were set up where students could air their grievances and learn to better understand what led to the outbreak of violence.

The whole episode was a learning experience for all of us. I recall Margie telling me about the discussion groups she participated in. As she put it, "I guess I can't blame them for rioting or being upset. The black kids complain about having to ride on the bus for two hours to get to school, coming from the slums they live in and passing through the uppity sections of Charlotte on the way to Myers Park High."

They also complained about militant blacks threatening their families if they didn't participate in demonstrations and activist plans. The militants incited the black folks by saying things like, "See how much better off the white people are. You think you will ever get to be where they are? No, there is no chance you'll ever get there in the present system."

All the airing of grievances resulted in a new awareness for our children, both of racial discrimination and social class divisions in our society, as well as how militant revolutionaries sometimes operate. The things our kids learned in the discussion groups they participated in really blew them away. On the whole, I think the police officer who led most of the discussions was good at what he did. Our kids couldn't say enough good things about him.

Racial tensions persisted for awhile in Charlotte. Chris was in junior high school and already a popular athlete. About ten black students jumped him one day at school and beat him up. He ended up with a broken nose. Chris was still in shock about it all when he arrived home.

"Chris, what happened?" I demanded to know.

"Mom, I have no idea," he told me. "These were fellows I play with on different sports teams. I thought they were my friends."

A police officer, who happened to be black, met with me afterward to determine the best course of action to take in responding to the assault on Chris. The officer had the names of all those involved in the altercation. He also knew there was a ringleader, someone who had, again, been influenced by some of the militant groups trying to stir up trouble in Charlotte.

The civil rights movement was a complex social upheaval, particularly in southern societies. We were all well acquainted with Martin Luther King, Jr., and his non-violent efforts to get discriminatory laws and practices changed. I had no problem supporting his work. Many of us welcomed the changes. But there were other groups not willing to restrict themselves to non-violent means of protest. Of course there were organized groups among white folks as well, equally willing to resort to violence to preserve the status quo. It was a difficult time to raise kids, difficult to know how to talk to them and get them to understand all that was happening, and to keep them from growing to hate and adopt racist attitudes.

The police officer suggested we not press charges against those who had assaulted Chris, particularly the ringleader of the group, saying if he spent time in prison, which he would have, he would turn out ten times more hateful and violent than he already was. The officer asked for my cooperation in getting the attackers into a counseling program. They would all be arrested, then in a plea-bargaining deal be required to attend counseling sessions. The officer said he would personally be working with them in the sessions.

I was impressed with what he had to say and I liked the approach he was taking. I also saw it as an opportunity to teach my own kids how best to respond to acts of racism. I spoke to Chris about it and he was relieved. As he put it, "Mom, it will only get worse if you have the ringleader arrested. I don't know what would happen, but it would not be good."

In the end it was a good lesson for all of us in learning to respond to an act of racial hatred by taking a course of action we believed would be most helpful.

I don't know how much my being "black" for a short while when I was a young girl influenced my thinking, but the experience was certainly in the back of my mind during those years of change. I remembered how people looked at me, judged me because of the color of my skin, and thought I should be sitting in the back of the bus. I learned a lot from the experience. And I've learned from helpful discussions I've had with black people over the years about the prejudices they face.

I know since we've had our own business, we've been strict about treating employees equally. Everyone has the same rules to follow, and if a person shows up and does his or her job effectively, he or she will be judged on performance, not skin color. And if we get employees who display any kind of racial prejudice, they don't stay with us very long. I feel strongly about these policies.

What still intrigues me, however, is how I liked the dark skin color I got from lying out in the sun. I just didn't like the assumptions people made about me for having dark skin.

Chapter Seventeen

WORKING WOMAN

I have had many women in business come to me and ask how I managed to succeed as a businesswoman. I have to say, what I learned before Ron and I went into business for ourselves was as important as anything I learned since. Much of it has to do with developing a good work ethic, but I also learned early in my working career to be a contributor in creative and thoughtful ways, and how to communicate my ideas effectively.

I learned from watching my father while I was growing up that working twelve to fourteen hours a day is normal if a person wants to succeed. And he wasn't the only one. Most of the adult men I knew were family friends who were Greek, and most of them were in the restaurant business. They all worked like my father. I learned what it took to get ahead from watching them.

Without a doubt, my daddy's influence on me early on, from when he would let me sit up by the cash register and take the money from customers in the restaurant to when I started working as a waitress, taught me to think of work as a meaningful part of life. Work was not just a forty-hour segment of each week we have to endure in order to get a paycheck. Imbibing the energy and passion my father had for his work, the creativity he put into his cooking, and the manner in which he identified himself with his restaurant made a lasting impression on me.

Daddy was a "go get em, Kat" person. I remember once when I was eight or nine years old, getting in a neighborhood spat during a ballgame.

I hit a young boy who was bothering me, then took off running. I climbed a tree right next to our house to get away from him, even though I was wearing a skirt. He climbed up after me, but he couldn't climb up as far as I was willing to go. So he started shaking the tree. I started yelling for my grandmother because I was slipping. I ended up falling onto another branch and scraping the skin off the insides of my legs.

Grandma ran the kid off, then she proceeded to give me hell in Hungarian before she calmed down enough to switch to English and let me know, "Ladies do not climb trees. Ladies do not fight. You are not a boy. You are a girl." In the end, my mother sided with Grandmother, but my Daddy let me know he was proud of me for sticking up for myself.

My early role models were all males. I was raised with two brothers. The kids I played with as a child were all boys. At that time in history it was taken for granted that men were going to be the primary breadwinners for families and the ones most likely to have ambitions to succeed in business enterprises. Somehow the distinction didn't register with me. Boys and men were just a more dominant influence in my early life than females were. I learned to be a go-getter from them.

I was always out playing softball or touch football with the neighborhood boys. I participated in sports when I was in high school. Knowing how to be single-minded in pursuit of a goal is something playing on a ball team cultivates in a person, as well as an aggressive spirit. That is why it is so important to have young girls active in sporting programs if women are going to advance in the business world.

When I went to work as a thirteen-year-old at Belk's department store, and then moved on to Sears, and then to the Bank of Charlotte when I was still a teenager, I not only learned to assume responsibility, but to enjoy being a part of a work environment and to be committed to getting the job done.

I always felt I was as capable as anybody else and the opportunities were there for me to succeed if I just worked at it. Yes, there was a male bias. I recall that, later on when I worked uptown at Wachovia Bank, there were no female customer service managers, no branch managers who were female, and no women in upper management positions. I once made a comment to my male colleagues, suggesting "Someday, that is all going to change."

They became defensive, and one fellow wanted to know, "What makes you so sure?"

"Because the banks are going to get tired of paying you guys these big salaries," I said. "They will find out women will do the job just as well for less."

And that is exactly what happened.

When it came to any kind of sexual harassment, I was quick to assert myself and put a stop to it. Even when I was young, working my first bank job at the Bank of Charlotte, I was willing to stand up for myself.

There was this fellow working at the bank who I had been warned to watch out for. He would walk along behind the tellers on his way to the bank vault. I was at the end, just before the vault. As he would walk by he would wave his arm a bit and then let it fall as he was passing behind me such that his hand would bounce off my fanny. "Oops, excuse me," he would say.

This only happened a few times before I spoke up. "Don't do that again," I told him.

He looked at me and asked, "Do what?"

"You know what you did," I said. "Just don't do it again."

Then he asked me, "Do you know who I am?"

"Yes, I know who you are, but I am going to repeat what I said as nice as I can. Don't do it again."

Of course, he wanted to know what I would do if he didn't stop.

I proceeded to tell him, "Either I'll slap your face or I'll go to the president."

He just laughed. "Your job will become miserable," he said.

I reported the incident to the president the next morning, telling him, "I'm here at the risk of losing my job or becoming miserable with my job. I'm not sure which."

"Katherine, my God. You are one of the best we have ever had here," he said.

"Thank you. I appreciate that," I replied, "but I don't know if I can continue working here because I have been threatened."

The president was all ears at that point and wanted to know all the details.

I didn't see the young fellow at work the rest of the day. He showed up the next morning and asked for a chance to speak to me in private in the vault. I wasn't about to go in the vault with him, but agreed to go off to one corner. He then proceeded to apologize to me and offer a few feeble excuses. I questioned his sincerity, but from then on he went around in front of the tellers when he needed to get to the vault and left me alone.

Wherever I worked, I always tried to do more than was expected of me. After Ron and I moved back to Charlotte and before the loss of our first child, I became employed at the Federal Reserve here in Charlotte. My first job there was processing money orders. In those days money orders were cards, and we had a machine we ran them through to process them. I used to race the machine. And I was forever having to wait on the machine.

My supervisor came up to me one day and said, "Katherine, you are going to kill this machine."

"Well, it doesn't go fast enough," I told him. "Is there not a way to make it go faster?"

He looked at me a bit astonished, and replied, "I've never had anyone ask to make a machine go faster."

"Please do," I said, "because I could process more cards if the machine went faster."

He had a technician come in and work on the machine to get it to go a little faster.

A little later I graduated to processing Federal Reserve checks. Again, I worked at a machine, this time one that had buttons on one side directing the checks to be sent out to various regions. I had to read the address on the check, then press the appropriate button. Again, I could go faster than the machine, so much so that the checks began to clog up in the sorting process.

I was told, "Katherine, you are going to have to slow down."

"It's just my nature. I want to get through," was my response.

I also married a man who doesn't mind being called a workaholic. He thinks workaholics are the ones who make America great. "They are the ones," he likes to say, "who provide jobs and financial security for the rest of the population." From the early years of our marriage, he would be off to work at 6:00 a.m. and often not get home until ten or eleven at night.

I was almost always supportive of Ron's ambitions. He loved his work. And I would always take an interest in what he was doing. Too many women understand little about their husband's job. They aren't interested. They don't ask questions and talk about what is happening in their husband's workplace. Big mistake, in my opinion.

I could handle Ron's work habits because I had grown up watching my father put in long hours, but also because, by taking an interest in knowing what he was doing, I felt a part of the effort.

Success requires more than just hard work, however. One has to think creatively and be bold enough to venture new possibilities. I learned a valuable lesson in how important making positive suggestions can be when I was working part-time for the People's Bank in Greensville, South Carolina. The experience really helped to shape my identity in the workplace.

This was around 1960. I was working at a small branch office of the bank. Being a part-timer, I was low person on the totem pole. Still, I began to note a lot of things being done that I felt were ineffective. Some that I noted were procedural routines, others were rules we had to abide by that I thought were just plain wrong.

I discussed the matter with Ron and he told me, "Complaining is not going to change a thing, because everyone complains. Why don't you make a list of areas needing attention, then alongside your points, offer suggestions for what could be done."

I thought he had a good approach. He had learned this idea from having attended a Dale Carnegie course. And there is a lot to be said for it. Don't just turn in a list of complaints; include positive contributions toward a solution.

I went to work over the next couple of weeks writing out a list on a legal-size writing pad. By the time I was done, I had two-and-a-half pages full of ideas. I showed what I had done to Ron. He liked it.

Then came the part requiring a bit of courage. I took the document to work and told the branch manager what I had done, then showed him my list of perceived problems and suggestions.

He quickly perused the list and handed the document back to me, then said, "You really want to get fired, don't you? You try to tell the bank management what to do and you are going to get yourself fired."

I stood my ground and politely answered, "No, I don't want to be fired, but I don't want to work for a bank that won't take any suggestions on how to improve things."

I didn't drop the matter there. I took the initiative and called Phil Hungerford, vice president of the Bank. He was more open and said, "Sure, Katherine, bring it down to me and let's have a look at what you've done."

On my next day off from work I went downtown to the main branch of the bank. The building was all marble, with large marble columns out front—a foreboding place, particularly for a twenty-six year old part-time employee stepping forward to make suggestions on how to change some basic operations.

The vice president, Mr. Hungerford, was someone Ron knew through his work, and he had helped me get a job at the bank. He welcomed me into his office, seated me, and made sure I was comfortable. I gave him the document I had prepared, thinking he would accept it and put it in some pile to look at later. I was surprised when he went to work reading it right then and there. I was a bit nervous, and I appreciated when he would break the silence and ask me for a little clarification on some points I had made. But he continued, carefully reading through the entire two-and-a-half pages.

When he finished he looked up and said, "This is good. Would you mind if I keep this?"

Needless to say I felt a big sense of relief, but I answered, saying, "I'm flattered you would want to keep it."

"No, you have some pretty dog-gone good ideas in here," he said. "And I agree with you. We need to get up to date, get into the 20th century."

The next day I went back to work at the branch office. I had told the branch manager what I intended to do, and he had told the five other employees who worked at the branch I would probably be fired. He was surprised to see me back at work.

"Did you take it in?" he asked me,

"Yes," I said.

"Who did you give it to?" he wanted to know.

When I told him he said, "Oh, Katherine," and turned around and walked off.

The other bank employees got a chuckle out of our exchange. Then one of them said to me, "You know, he's right."

Well, I didn't care. Losing my job at the bank wouldn't have been the end of the world for me. I would not have appreciated being fired, but I could get over it. More importantly, I didn't want to work for a closed-minded company.

The matter was dropped afterward for a few weeks. Nobody said anything about it. But once a month we had to go down to the main branch to pull all the statements needing to be mailed out to our customers. We'd go through and confirm all the checks against the statements, put everything in an envelope, and mail the contents to each customer.

We were on our way down to the main branch when one of the head tellers asked me, "Have you heard anything about the suggestions you put in?"

"Nope," I replied.

"Well, you're still here, so somebody must have lost them."

"So be it, then," I replied, "but if I see the vice president I gave them to, I'll ask him."

We went straight up to the statements room when we arrived, so there was little chance of me seeing the vice president. His office was on the other side of the building.

We worked until about eight thirty that night and as the four of us, including the branch manager, were leaving, we heard somebody call out behind us, "Mrs. Harper."

The voice echoed all over the marble hallway of the bank. Our branch manager looked and said to me, "It's the president of the bank. Goodbye."

One of the other tellers turned to me and said, "Katherine, it's been good knowing you."

I was shaking. It *was* the president.

I walked back to where he was standing and he said to me, "I'm glad to meet you." Then he extended his hand for me to shake. "Would you mind coming into my office?"

I followed him into his office and he told me to have a seat right in front of his desk. Then he reached into a drawer in his desk and pulled out three familiar-looking sheets of legal paper.

"I understand you did this," he said.

"Yes, sir," I meekly replied.

He paused a bit before continuing, "It must have taken a lot of time and thought to do all this?."

"Yes, sir, it did."

He held the sheets up so I could see them and asked, "Do you see these little checkmarks along the side?"

Just about every line on the list had a checkmark in front of it, and many of them had two check marks.

Then he said, "The ones with two check marks, those we've already changed. The ones that have one check mark are going to take more time, but we are going to change them. Just about every suggestion you made on these two-and-a-half pages is going to be implemented."

I sat there, more than a bit flabbergasted, before asking, "Serious?"

"I want to tell you," he said, "how much we appreciate what you took the time and effort to do. I wish more employees would take this kind of interest."

He reached down to the front drawer of his desk and pulled out an envelope and handed it to me saying, "To show you our appreciation, I'd like to give you this."

I opened it to find a check for $350.00.

This was in 1960, when $350.00 was a lot of money, more than two months pay for a part-timer like me.

I was absolutely shocked. We stood up and I was shaking. The bank president noted my shaking and said, "Oh, by the way, I have someone to walk you out to your car."

Everyone else had already left.

"You'll calm down and you'll be all right," he added. "And if you come up with any more suggestions, let me know."

I just floated out of there.

I couldn't wait to get home. Ron met me at the door, and I was already blurting out, "Look! Look! Look!"

This was just prior to Christmas. We didn't have much money in those days, with four children. That check was a big blessing.

Next, I couldn't wait to get to work in the morning. I had asked the president if he minded if I showed the check to my branch manager, relating how he had said I would get fired.

"Is it that bad?" the president had inquired.

And I told him, "Yes, there is a lot of fear about saying anything needs to be changed. And you don't know how intimidating it is to come downtown and enter this big, imposing building that has been around so long. No one in the branch offices thinks he or she can have any influence on a well-established institution like this one."

He was reassuring. "You help spread the word," he said. "Show your branch manager the check if you wish."

I arrived at work early the next day. The first thing someone said to me was, "Are you here to get your things?"

"Nope," I said, "not at all." Then I reached in my pocketbook, pulled out the check I'd been given, and showed it to everyone.

They were incredulous! They just could not believe it.

In the weeks and months following, as I started seeing some of my suggestions being implemented, I tried my best to put into practice something else I think is key to being successful. I didn't take credit for the changes and improvements. I didn't even let others know it

I started out working as a bank teller at age seventeen and worked part-time much of the time I was raising a family. Later, in 1983, I was appointed by the Governor to the State Banking Commission. Here I am being sworn in by Appeals Court Judge Willis P. Whichard, along with other members on the board.

was my idea to do things the new way. When opportunities arose, I gave others the credit.

People don't realize how important this is. Needing to claim all the credit in an egocentric manner communicates to others that they are not significant and their help is not appreciated. To succeed, you have to have the help of other people, and the more you can make others feel their contribution is important, the more they will be motivated to participate in achieving goals. Too many people in business fail to realize this.

A few months after I received the $350.00 check, I had one more big suggestion to make to the bank management. This was something else that significantly contributed to my learning to be a successful businessperson. Ron had attended one of the Dale Carnegie courses on effective management and had come away from the experience excited about all he had learned. He was so enthused about the material that he was asked to work as a graduate assistant in the next course taught. He got me all excited about wanting to take the course too, but Ron's company wasn't going to pay for me to take the program, and I doubted very much whether People's Bank would pay for me to attend the fourteen-week, one-night-a-week course.

The fellow who taught the course was named Walt Farrar. I met him when Ron was graduating from the course and later expressed my interest to him, telling him how much I thought some of the bank managers could benefit from his instruction. His response was, "How about seeing if you can get me in the door?"

Not one to sit on my hands, I telephoned Mr. Hungerford, the vice president of the bank, and told him about the Dale Carnegie course and what a great instructor Walt was.

He thought a bit and asked me, "Katherine, what do you think?"

"Well," I said, "there are some people in the bank who would really like to have the benefit of taking this course."

Then I added, "And Walt wants me to take the course too, though I doubt if it will be possible for the bank to pay for me." I was still just a lowly part-timer, after all.

Mr. Hungerford responded by saying, "Have Walt give me a call."

A week went by and I sort of forgot about the matter. Then on Friday, I looked up from my work at the bank and saw Walt coming in the door. He was smiling from ear to ear.

"Katherine," he said. "Guess what?"

"I don't know. What?"

"He approved for you and five others to go, and he wants you to prepare the list of who the other five are. So you need to think about this."

I knew of two at my local branch who I wanted to go and maybe two at the main branch office downtown. I had to do a little work, but I came up with a list of managers and assistant managers who I thought could use a boost. These were guys who, when a customer came in the door, never moved from their chairs. I always thought they should get up to greet the customers, shake their hands, mingle with them, make them feel welcomed.

I checked with each one to make sure he wanted to take the course. Most of them laughed and told me, "Yeah, we want to see how you perform in the course."

There were about forty people in the class. I was really nervous at the start. Ron didn't prepare me in advance. He didn't give away what was going to happen. He wanted me to experience it the way he did.

The first night we were told we had to learn the names of all the others taking the class. We didn't think it was possible. Nearly everyone has trouble remembering people's names.

Walt, in his enthusiastic manner, explained to us why remembering people's names can be so important. People are flattered and feel significant when others remember their names the second time they meet them. When running a business, it makes a great impression on people.

But Walt also explained to us how we could learn, and remember, forty people's names in one night. You have to focus on hearing the name correctly, and then associate the person with someone else you know who has the same name, or with something else the name reminds you of.

Everyone in the class stood up and introduced themselves, then told a little about themselves. When everyone finished, each one of us were called upon to stand up and name everyone in the room. About half the class got 100 percent that night. I was one of them.

I was hooked on the course right from the start. I just loved the basic philosophy behind what we were being taught, namely, that we have so much potential within us that we don't exercise. We were learning what we already knew and could already do. We were just being taught to bring out the hidden potential.

There was so much I learned from the Dale Carnegie course. I especially benefited from the instruction in public speaking. We were taught always to speak on a topic we know something about and never try to address something we can't speak about from the heart, whether it has to do with business or whatever. One has to believe it in order to present a view persuasively.

Then we were instructed to never write a speech out. It is better to work from an outline of key words and phrases. Writing a speech out ties a person to the manuscript and inhibits natural spontaneity.

These lessons on public speaking went further when we had to give a speech while some of the others in the class were told to try to be as distracting as possible, by pounding on the table and waving their arms. We learned we could do it, staying focused on what we wanted to communicate despite whatever heckling we might encounter. I tell you, I learned so much.

I watched as the five fellows I had chosen to take the course turned absolutely around and became incredibly effective communicators. They were really helped by the course. It helped me, too. Without all that I learned at the Dale Carnegie course, I wouldn't have been able to take up many of the leadership roles I was able to assume later on. I learned I could stand up in a committee meeting or gathering and feel what I have to say is valuable. I learned how to communicate my ideas effectively and how not to allow myself to be rattled by opposition. This was such valuable training.

Three of those who graduated from the Dale Carnegie course I took were chosen to be graduate assistants. I was one of them, along with one of the fellows I'd selected from the bank to attend.

Several months later Walt called me up to tell me about plans for the new "Dorothy Carnegie" course, a program just for women. This was going to be geared toward motivating and providing skills for women pursuing careers in the business world. What's more, Walt told me he had nominated me for training to be an instructor for the course.

Walt must have heard me take a deep breath, because he asked, "What's the matter, aren't you interested?"

"No," I said, "I am really interested, except for one thing. I just found out I am pregnant again."

About eight months later I gave birth to our daughter Georgia. I think I would have loved teaching the course, and I think I would have been good at it. They would have wanted to fly me all over the country to do seminars. Still, just knowing I had been nominated for the position and knowing Walt thought I was that good was a big added boost to the confidence I had in my own abilities.

In so many ways, I felt prepared when the time came for the challenge of launching our own company, something Ron was becoming impatient to do.

The dedication of our new corporate headquarters in 1985. Shown left to right, myself, Mayor Harvey Gantt and Governor Jim Hunt

Chapter Eighteen

HARPER CORPORATION OF AMERICA

*T*he best way Ron learns is by diving in and going through an experience. I generally just pray we will survive. And we always have. At age thirty-eight Ron was growing frustrated working for other people and was increasingly confident and eager to go into business for himself. I completely supported him in the effort, but I did a lot of praying as well.

We founded Ron Harper Associates, Ltd. in 1971. I kept my day job at Wachovia Bank so we would have some income to fall back on and kept track of the financial side of the new business part-time. Ron went to work on a phone in an office we set up in a back room in our home, selling unengraved printing press rollers to customers he had been dealing with in his former jobs, taking orders, and ordering the production of rollers from machine shops. His plan was to stay out of production himself, wanting to do the marketing and writing up orders, then letting others do the manufacturing to the necessary specifications.

Surviving in the new enterprise required a lot of determination and hard work. We lost money at first and had to squeeze to get by. For three years we didn't take a vacation. There was no way we could have afforded one. We explained what we were doing to the kids, telling them how we had to put our home on the line to secure bank loans.

Our youngest, Georgia, who was ten at the time, asked, "If we lose the house, would that mean we'd move into an apartment that had a swimming pool?"

I remember smiling to myself as we answered, "Yes."

"Oh boy!" was her response.

If that was the worst that could happen, things couldn't be so bad, I concluded.

Finding ways to innovate proved to be the road to success for us. It wasn't long before we found ourselves launching into a series of developments that revolutionized the flexographic printing industry. A key feature on flexographic printing presses is what is known as an anilox roll, basically an ink transfer roller. We became involved in manufacturing a superior type of anilox roll. And within a few years we grew into a leading international competitor in the field of anilox roll production.

The first innovation we implemented was in applying a ceramic coating to the rollers we used, replacing the chrome coating that was popular at the time. The technology was first developed by the military, which was using "thermal flame spray" guns to apply molten ceramic to the nose cones of missiles. The result was a much harder and more durable ceramic coating, capable of withstanding extremely high temperatures.

A company out west discovered such a coating could be precisely engraved with the kind of finely dimpled surface needed on anilox rolls to pick up and transfer ink in the printing process. But that company failed to capitalize on the idea and effectively market it. Ron immediately recognized the potential value of the innovation and went to work seeking ways to develop it. We offered to form a partnership with the company out west, where that company would do the manufacturing and Ron would market the product. Failing there, Ron began seeking someone locally who provided the required thermal flame spray applications.

Almost by accident he discovered a new company right here in Charlotte using the technique to coat valves and pipes and other items to prevent rust and corrosion. We signed a contract with that outfit to coat the rollers Ron ordered from machine shops, and to mechanically engrave the rollers after they were coated. But not everything went smoothly.

We had been trying to stay out of manufacturing. Ron wanted to focus on utilizing his strengths in marketing. But problems kept coming up. Rollers were getting damaged during transport from the machine shops to the company doing the ceramic coating and engraving. We ended up having to purchase a truck and take over responsibility for inspecting the rollers and transferring them. Some of these were large, heavy rollers, requiring us to acquire lifting equipment to get them on and off the truck. Ron's brother Dick joined us and did some of this transfer work early on.

Quality control issues began to arise as well. The rollers weren't being produced to our specifications. And the company doing the ceramic coating didn't want to grow with our growth. When a larger lathe was needed to do the work, the company owner didn't want to invest the money.

I am the one who urged that we take over the manufacturing ourselves, knowing I would be the one who would do much of the day-to-day oversight of the effort. I could see Ron getting excited about finding a building, ordering equipment, starting the process, but after the interesting stuff was done, he would want someone else to run the operation so he could focus on what he did best, namely marketing. Which was fine with me. I was willing, with Dick's help, to oversee the production side.

Ron's bother Dick, who helped us with manufacturing in the first few years after we started our own business. I used to say he had nuts and bolts for brains, a compliment, 1975.

There was so much I still had to learn to get started, though I had always taken an interest in Ron's work. There were times I accompanied him to Atlanta and Texas to attend Flexographic Technical Association conferences and learn more about the industry. I used to love it.

What we were getting into was an extension of what Ron had done before. He taught me much of what he knew, including a practical, hands-on side to the manufacturing process. I can't say I ever operated a lathe, but I learned the basics of lathe operation and what we needed from a lathe operator. Ron also taught me the finer points in evaluating the quality of anilox roll engraving. He had a real talent for doing this. He could look at the surface on a roller after it was engraved and know what quality of a print job it would produce. He could run his hand across the surface and say, "Yep, it's good. That can go."

I learned to be able to do the same myself. I loved learning how things operated and I mastered the ins and outs of the production process, as well as staying on top of the financial side of the business.

In 1975 we opened a manufacturing plant in an old building on Crompton Street in Charlotte. About the same time we changed the name of the business to Harper Corporation of America. Ten years later, having greatly expanded our production capacities, we moved to the company's current location on Steel Creek Road in southwest Charlotte.

As I said, Ron's brother Dick joined us and assisted in managing the manufacturing side of the business in the early years. I used to say he had nuts and bolts for a brain, not to denigrate him, but meaning he was very bright when it came to dealing with anything mechanical.

The first day he went to work with us, Ron sent Dick out to Gastonia, where some company was having problems getting their printing press to work right. Dick had never worked on a printing press before in his life, but it didn't take him long to figure out how and why something on the press was out of alignment. He had it fixed in no time and the press operators were impressed. One of them asked him, "How long have you been with Harper Corporation?"

"All day," he responded.

Ron and I watching an anilox roll turn in a lathe in a photo taken for an article in the old *Charlotte News* newspaper, 1975.

Dick was a big help to us when we were first getting the company rolling. He eventually spun off his own company, called Harper Machinery Corporation.

In the meantime, much happened to transform Harper Corporation of America. One early development I had a direct role in proved to be a big success and provided a reliable flow of revenue to keep us afloat during our early years in business.

The first few times I accompanied Ron out to visit some of the customers we sold anilox rolls to I was appalled at how filthy their equipment was. These customers were mostly what are known in the industry as "converters," people who produce the packaging materials for products. Most of the labels printed on packaging materials are printed using flexographic presses. And the presses I was seeing looked like nobody ever bothered to clean them.

"Oh my God, it's filthy," I would say.

And Ron would answer, "Shh, don't say that out loud."

"But Ron, it is why they are having trouble getting good quality prints."

"I know," he said, "but you don't tell them because it won't do any good. What we have to do is give them a solution to the problem."

What was needed was some kind of cleaning formula that could clean the ink off the presses and especially off the anilox rolls. As it was, ink was drying in the little dimples on the surface of the rollers and reducing the amount of ink transferred, drastically changing the print quality. Cleaning these rollers with the solvents then available was a nasty job, and nothing was working well.

I was still working at the bank at the time. One of the customers who regularly made deposits was the owner of a chemical plant. I knew him well because we often conversed when he came in. So I asked him if he thought he could come up with a cleaning solution that would not be caustic yet would dissolve the kind of inks used in flexography after the ink had dried. He agreed to experiment some and see what he could do.

Ron took him some small anilox rollers which he had really gunked up with ink and let dry. The fellow worked on the project for just a short time before he came up with a formula that worked wonderfully. We named the new cleaning solution " CeramClean™," and quickly started marketing it. The formula was an instant hit. A converter only needed to clean his roller in the press with a rag, or build a tank and fill it with the solution, then soak the rollers and any other pieces of equipment in the solution to have the dry ink melt away.

The chemical manufacturer produced the stuff and put it in fifty-gallon drums. We would receive orders and have him ship out the drums. The money we made off CeramClean kept us going in the early years and gave us needed funds to allow us to expand.

The next big innovation we successfully implemented was the use of laser beams to do the engraving on anilox rolls. Prior to this the dimpled surfaces on the rollers were produced by pressing a small wheel-shaped engraving tool against a roller as it turned in a lathe. Precision in the alignment was essential, and the result would be perfectly lined up, diamond-shaped dimples on the surface of the roller.

One of our biggest competitors, a company named Pamarco, successfully experimented with using a laser beam to do this engraving.

The laser beam directed at a roller would pulsate as the roller turned in a lathe-like piece of equipment. The intense heat of the laser beam would melt the ceramic surface of the roller each time a pulse was emitted, just enough to leave a little dimple. With the lathe-like machine continuing to turn the roller, the pulsating laser beam slowly and precisely moved down the length of the roller, producing an engraved roller.

Ron immediately recognized the potential of this development and started looking into utilizing it. At the time, Pamarco, the first company to use lasers to engrave anilox rolls, seemed content to mostly continue engraving the old, mechanical way. Ron saw the chance to leap ahead, taking advantage of the increased precision of the new technology, as well as drawing recognition to Harper Corporation for advancing this innovation.

Two of our sons, Jimmy and Chris, were working for us at the time. Neither one of them had any training in laser technology but they understood what was needed to produce anilox rolls and they understood equipment. We sent them over to Europe to visit a couple of laser manufacturers. They came back having been most impressed with an inventor/manufacturer in England who was willing to work with us to make the needed adaptations we wanted.

We had already been contemplating other innovations. Rather than using diamond shaped dimples, we had discussed the use of hexagonal, honeycomb, shaped dimples, which would be an even more efficient use of surface space. I had even dreamed about the honeycomb and woke up saying, "We need a honeycomb pattern."

The laser equipment was a big investment but one of the best moves we ever made. Our research on the use of the honeycomb pattern, as well as experiments on different dimple widths and depths was another revolution for the industry. Using laser engraving, we were able to engrave anilox rolls which had as many as two thousand dimples (cells) per linear inch. Since in flexographic printing the anilox roll transfers the ink onto the printing plate, with each little dimple placing a tiny dot of ink on the plate, the quality of the anilox roll is mostly responsible for the quality of the finished print. By increasing the number of dimples per inch, enhancing the layout of the dimples with the honeycomb pattern, and increasing the efficiency of ink transfer by optimizing dimple depths, we dramatically increased the quality of flexographic printing. Flexographic printing, long considered lower-end printing, now competes with offset printing for quality, and does so at a lower cost.

We caused a revolution in the industry when we came out with plasma flame spray ceramic coatings on anilox rolls. Laser engraving, plus the research that led to the honeycomb pattern and optimized cell depth and width on anilox rolls, furthered the dramatic changes occurring in the industry. These innovations, together with our more recent development of an enhanced ceramic coating on what we call our "platinum anilox rolls" have been the basis for the international reputation Harper Corporation has developed in the flexographic printing industry.

Ron used to say it was an amazing coincidence that these major developments—thermal flame spray technology and laser engraving —came together just as we were beginning to build a company. I never saw it as coincidence. In my view, our success was not due largely to coincidence. Maybe it was the grace of God, plus plenty of energetic effort on our part.

We are not scientists. I was not even brought up around mechanics or manufacturing. But we keep abreast of developments in the field by attending trade shows and seminars and reading trade journals. And we are good at recognizing good ideas, capable of feeling a good fit and knowing when some new development will work. We also encourage innovative thinking among our employees. We tell them, "If you know of a better way to approach a problem or develop something new, by all means." The results have paid off for us.

Besides manufacturing anilox rolls, we have come out with other product lines. We formed a partnership, Harper/Love Adhesives Corporation, with an Australian company and have for many years produced and marketed an adhesive additive that is used in the making of corrugated cardboard. We also manufactured metering rollers and glue applicator rollers.

Ron on one of the many cruises we have gone on, this one in 1985.

My major contribution to the success of Harper Corporation of America over the years was in overseeing the manufacturing side of the business and keeping tabs on the financial end. Manufacturing was always my heart. I knew I would never get any control over sales, and I didn't really want to. Ron is the best there is in that department.

In managing the manufacturing I didn't do any direct supervising of work on the shop floor, but I did get to know our employees and I stayed on top of what the supervisors were thinking and doing. I can identify with the working class people because Ron was one of them during the early years of our marriage. He was a laborer when he started out. I used to make it a point to go out and personally meet each new employee. I liked to talk with people and get to know them, to learn about their families. The first time I would shake hands. After I got to know them, I would tell them to expect to get hugged. If I didn't hug them, they would want to know what was wrong. The workers in the plant still like to call me "Mrs. H." I don't know, but maybe it stands for "Mrs. Hugs."

Part of my responsibility in overseeing the manufacturing was in solving problems. If there was anything bad going on, it was my job to straighten the situation out. For example, there was a time when we were having problems with tools and machine parts being stolen from out of the shop. Costs were going up as a result. We were losing a basic trust between employer and employee.

"We can solve the problem," I proposed. "We'll build cages to lock the tools up in. Employees will have to check out the tools they work with and check them back in at the end of the day." People complained, saying my solution would further undermine trust. But I wasn't afraid to speak directly to the shop hands, telling them what was in store if things didn't stop disappearing.

A little later I received a tip. Someone phoned to suggest I check behind the trash bins at the back of the plant fifteen minutes after closing. So I sauntered out onto the loading dock in the back that afternoon. As I was getting ready to jump down off the dock to check behind the trash bins, one of our employees suddenly appeared and said, "What are you doing, Mrs. Harper?"

I said, "There is some trash out here I need to check out."

"Oh, I'll do that," he said.

"No," I responded, "I'll do it."

There behind the trash bins was a pile of brand new sanding belts, the kind we use to polish rollers before engraving them. One of the employees was selling these and other items to another company up the road.

I learned to crack down on problems of this nature, and I got the reputation of being the bad guy. I know the supervisors would tell employees, "She's tough. When you hear a change in the tone of her voice, you know you are in trouble. However, she is fair, and she will never do anything that will harm you if you don't deserve it."

Tracking down shenanigans in other departments was equally important. We had an attorney working for us who, unbeknown to us, had contracted with a law firm to restructure our corporation. It appeared to us, once we learned about the scheme, that he was attempting to siphon off profits from our international sales. The whole plan came to light when he was out of town one week and an invoice arrived from the law firm he was working with. I asked Ron if he knew anything about it. Ron had never heard of the law firm. When we contacted the firm drafting the legal documents, they claimed they couldn't believe we knew nothing about the restructuring. We immediately squelched that situation.

We hired a chemist to oversee experiments we were conducting on inks and other products we were developing. He worked for us for about three years before I grew suspicious about items on handwritten invoices from a particular supplier. Our purchasing agent claimed he knew nothing about what was happening because the chemist, who was also managing the department, did all the ordering. I called the supplier in question and asked why we were being charged for items we don't use or market. At first I received evasive answers, until I threatened to cut off our orders from him. Only then did he reveal that our chemist was running his own business on the side and deliveries were being made to his home, with the bills being sent to us.

He was clever, and some people may think we are so nice we just might be stupid.

"We weren't born yesterday," I told him when I fired him. It might take a bit to catch up with someone like him, but things come out eventually.

Not all the shenanigans occurring in the company were attempts at graft. There are tricks of the trade accountants use to make themselves look good. The first person who really taught me accounting told me what to be on the lookout for.

We had an accounting supervisor who was always trying to keep the bottom line looking good. One of the tricks frequently employed is to use the other person's money as long as possible, meaning not paying the bills until it is absolutely necessary. This is not how we normally operate. There are some vendors who would give us a 10 percent discount if we paid them in ten days. But our accountant wasn't taking advantage of such savings.

I began getting suspicions when opening the mail at the beginning of the month and finding "past due" and "cut off" stamped on invoices. I asked our purchasing agent what was going on. He told me that we had already been cut off by some companies. "The bills aren't getting paid," he said.

Now, it wasn't a matter of us not having funds available. Cash flow at that point was good and we even had a reserve fund to dip into. But our accountant kept telling me, "Everything is fine. Don't worry about it. There is no need to use the reserves."

I went to the bookkeeper after opening the mail and finding all the "past due" notices. She told me, "We write checks for them, but the checks don't get mailed. They are sitting in the supervisor's drawer."

She showed me his drawer, and sure enough, it was full of bills and checks ready to go out. As the bookkeeper told me, the supervisor "was jockeying the books a little bit."

"A lot," I added.

About the same time I received a phone call from American Express. The woman on the phone was someone I knew from doing business with American Express over the years. She told me about our overdue payments and, as she put it, "We are shutting you down today."

It just so happened we had eight people attending a conference, covering all their expenses with American Express cards. They would have been left hanging, having to come up with some alternative way to pay for their rooms and all.

That is when things came to a head. I confronted the accounting supervisor about the matter. He wanted to know why I had been opening the mail.

"I beg your pardon," I replied.

It wasn't just American Express that was past due. There were $60,000 worth of unpaid bills. By holding off on recording and paying bills, the accountant made the bottom line look better. But he had been stretching his timing way too much.

I made a phone call to the bank and asked to have money transferred out of our reserve fund to cover expenses. We also had to send our past due payments to American Express by overnight mail to keep from having our accounts closed. The rest of the checks were mailed out. Needless to say, we went looking for another accounting supervisor.

When it comes to the financial costs of running a business, I learned when working in the bank to overestimate what actual costs are projected to be. All too often I saw people take out loans to cover some expense, and then come up short later on. So if someone tells me something is going to cost $50,000, in my mind I add a big surplus to that figure. There are always additional expenses beyond the ticket price of the item. In production, people think a figure will be close enough, and they don't anticipate other aspects or problems that might show up. Managers also often forget to calculate in the cost of lost time when changes are being made.

When approaching a bank for a loan, I have generally made it a practice to ask for more than we have estimated something will cost. If we are investing in a $50,000 piece of equipment, I'll ask for $80,000, just so we'll be sure to have enough to cover the unseen costs.

One other practice Ron and I have always been committed to is being completely honest about paying our taxes. We have always advised people who come to us asking about starting a business to make it a habit to pay taxes—state, federal, or whatever. Also, if you operate in a manner where you reinvest in your company, you will never have to dread being audited by the Internal Revenue Service.

We were once audited by an agent from the state. He spent a week pouring over our financial records. Finally I went and asked him how long he was going to keep investigating us.

He sort of laughed and said, "Mrs. Harper, I've got to tell you something. Every time I think I have caught Harper Corporation on some point, I see these little notes that send me somewhere else. And when I follow the lead, a suitable answer is given in the new place to resolve the issue. Who is writing all these little notes?"

"I don't know," I said. "Let me see what you are talking about."

He showed me one, and I told him, "That's my handwriting."

He showed me another, and I said, "That's me, too."

What he was finding was what I call "truth trails." I've tried to teach others to do the same thing, connecting relevant items together to clarify what has been done in various transactions.

"That's incredible," the auditor finally told me. "The only place I can find where you haven't paid taxes is on your magazine subscriptions. You've been deducting those and that is not permitted."

"They are all industrial magazines having to do with the industry," I protested. "We have to have them to be apprised on what is going on in the field of flexography."

"Sorry," he said. "But I'll tell you what I'll do. I'll make sure there is no fine or penalty."

Well, after a week-long audit, we were satisfied that all we had been found to be remiss in was magazine subscriptions.

When I wasn't running around putting out fires, there was always plenty for me to do as president of Harper Corporation of America. A reporter for The Charlotte News once wrote, "The (Harper) family business (has) benefited from good marital mixes: Katherine's money-handling skills and Ron's marketing expertise; Katherine's warmth and Ron's intensity." He was probably on to something.

Ron was never good at sitting through long meetings with attorneys, hammering out the specifics on contracts, or meeting with insurance agents and coming up with healthcare plans, and a thousand other decision-making processes required to keep a company going. I always handled the bulk of this side of the business, along with staying abreast of financial details and doing what it takes to secure bank loans.

Much of the day-to-day work of overseeing administration was my responsibility. Handling employees and dealing with employee relations came naturally to me. We always felt a key to success for any company hoping to succeed on the national and international level was the ability to attract and keep outstanding people. And we believed as long as we treated our employees as well as we treated our customers, we could keep them.

Over the years I tried to build more company spirit among employees by planning Christmas parties, then company picnics in the summer. First it was just a Christmas party, where employees could bring their spouses. Then we added a children's party, with Santa Claus and all. During one period when finances got tight, we cancelled the Christmas gathering for children. Word came to me that one of the children complained "Doesn't Mrs. Harper love us anymore?" Afterward we added the family picnic in the summer and kept the Christmas party for the adults in December. For me it was all a part of what made the job fun and interesting.

From the beginning, when we first went into business, Ron and I have regularly attended and been actively involved in the professional conferences for people in the industries we are associated with. One of the first conferences I went to was put on by the Technical Association of the Pulp and Paper Industry (TAPPI). There were about 750 men in attendance. I was the only female.

Ron, having worked selling anilox rolls before we formed our own company, knew most of the people there. Halfway through the conference this tall fellow walked up to Ron and I and shook hands with Ron.

Ron introduced him to me, saying, "This is Doug Tuttle. He works for Pamarco."

Pamarco was our biggest competitor.

"Well," Doug said to me, "I just came over to complain to Ron that he has to play fair."

Ron looked at him and asked, "What do you mean I don't play fair?"

"When it comes to advertising and marketing," he said.

"We are just getting started," Ron stammered. "We've been able to do very little."

"No," he said, "you brought Katherine here. She is the only female at this conference, and everyone is saying 'who is that woman?' And of course, when they ask, we have to tell them, 'That is Ron Harper's wife.' And then they ask, 'Who is Ron Harper?' And we have to tell them what you do, and now everyone here knows you are my competitor."

We all got a big laugh out of the exchange. And we generally enjoyed good relations with our competitors. But yes, I did enter a man's world when I joined Ron on the adventure of Harper Corporation of America. I think I've done a good job and, with our daughter Margie now taking over the reins of the company, I hope I've helped pave the way for other women in the industry.

It didn't take long before I was up to my neck in trade association affairs, first as a member of various committees and then as "chairman" of the corrugated division of the TAPPI international conference. I was also an officer and chairman of the printing committee for three years and served in various other positions.

I mentioned the way I like to hug people once I get to know them. I was raised that way and it is just part of my nature. We did have a manager once who objected to the way I would always be hugging people. I guess he thought it was unprofessional. "It just doesn't look right," he told me once.

The next time a flexography conference came around, we were there as usual. By that time there was a small handful of women who attended, but it was still very much a man's world. We had just arrived at the hotel and were checking in at the lobby. I noticed a group of men off to one side, old acquaintances of ours who we were used to seeing at conferences. I was inclined to go over and give them each a hug, but we had brought our young, new manager with us who had questioned my hugging habits. So I was feeling a little restrained.

I walked over to the group and said, "Hi, everybody. How you doing?"

They were all friendly and wanted to know how I was doing.

"I'm doing great," I said.

A little conversation started before one fellow said, "Wait a minute. Let's stop right here."

He looked at me before continuing. "Katherine, are you mad at us?"

A bit baffled, I replied, "No."

"Well," he asked, "why aren't you giving us a hug?"

I laughed and said, "Well, it's like this. Someone told me it wasn't appropriate for me to be hugging everyone."

Together, a couple of them said, "Tell us who it is and we'll kill him."

I turned around and pointed out our new manager and said, "It was him."

They yelled over at him, "You get out of here."

Then they turned back to me and said, "Now, Mrs. Harper, we want our hugs."

Chapter Nineteen

MOTHER'S LAST YEARS

I **had a difficult time** when my mother died on January 10, 1976. More than the grief I felt over not having her around anymore, it was knowing what she had to go through in the last years of her life that weighed so heavily on me.

After Father passed away on May 2, 1959, my brother George stepped up to assume the duties of the eldest son, saying he was going to take care of Mother.

"I'm taking her back to Florida with me," he assured me, "and she will never, ever have to worry about a roof over her head, the next meal, or anything. She will be able to come and go as she deserves, and have her own friends. She will be well taken care of for the rest of her days."

"That is wonderful," is all I could say in reply, as I hoped for the best.

When Daddy died he left Mother the house and the car. She took charge of selling just about everything in the house, then the house, in preparation for moving to Florida. She had no qualms about moving in with George, who was not married at the time and living by himself. The arrangement fit with her faith and belief that the eldest son should take care of his mother.

In preparation for her moving in, George rented a two-bedroom apartment, and when Mother arrived she used her money to buy extra furniture and other items she needed. She had always been so frugal, thinking of the children, counting her pennies, fearing Daddy might not approve of her purchases. For the first time in life she was free to spend money as she wished.

For more than a few years Mother got along fine. Living with George was working out well for her. We went down to visit occasionally. Even when George started dating a young woman, who we met and immediately liked, we thought things would continue to go smoothly for Mother.

Then one day, unexpectedly, George called to tell us he was bringing Mother home.

"What do you mean, 'bringing her home'?" I wanted to know.

He was preparing to bring her back to Charlotte. Much had been happening. He had broken up with the woman he had been dating and had starting seeing another woman. Mother didn't care for this second woman. Then George decided to move in with his new lady friend.

The change wasn't what Mother had been anticipating. She and George had discussed buying a home together and moving out of the apartment they were in. Now George's lady-friend, Eileen, was inviting them to move into her home. "You are welcome to move in as well," Mother was told.

Mother was from the old school. Living together unmarried was wrong in her mind, and she wasn't about to share the same home with two people living in sin. I don't think she really ever expected George would place his personal life before his duties to her, and she never got over it.

As for myself, I was delighted to hear Mother was moving back to Charlotte. "Mother, the kids will love having you around. We'll enjoy having you stay with us," I told her.

We fixed up a room with the kind of frilly curtains she loved and got her moved in.

But Mother was just not the same anymore. The sparkle had gone out of her eyes. Her dream had absolutely faded.

"It's not right," she would say. "George promised me, and now I'm going to be a burden to you."

"Mother, it is okay," I would assure her. "You are not a burden. It is actually a relief for me to have you here."

But she never could accept what had happened. She began to get steadily more depressed. I tried to get medical treatment for her, but the doctor I took her to wouldn't prescribe anything for depression, plus this was before most of the anti-depressant medications we now have were invented. "What does she have to be depressed about?" he would ask. "She is living with you. She has everything she needs."

He clearly didn't understand human psychology. "No, she doesn't have everything she needs," I argued. "She's going through a big disappointment concerning my oldest brother."

Still, I couldn't get the doctor to treat her for depression.

Mother brooded over George in the months following. "George is a lot like your daddy was," she would say. "I didn't realize he took on most of your daddy's faults."

I tried to get her to let it be. "George has been out on his own," I would say. "He's been independent for years. He lives his own life. And there is no woman, whether it is you or his current lady friend or anyone else who is going to tie him down."

All Mother could say was, "I don't understand it."

Matters took a strange turn when Mother received a letter from, of all people, Eileen, George's lady-friend, the one he had moved in with. Mother would not let me read the letter or tell me what it said, but I saw tears in her eyes after she read it. Afterward I took her along with me to the grocery store, hoping a little activity might lift her spirits. She passed out in the store. Very worried, I called the doctor. He told me to take her home, put her to bed, and bring her into his office the next day if she didn't improve. Her distress level was clearly growing.

I learned a bit later of the contents of the upsetting letter. As I recall, Eileen was angry at George and wrote all kinds of horrible things about him to Mother, apparently thinking she could once and for all break the relationship between George and his mother and end any obligations he still felt toward his mother. Most of what she wrote was not true, but Mother was too distraught to be able to figure it all out.

When Christmas came around, Mother's sister, my Aunt Edna, who continued to live in Charlotte, invited Mother to spend the holidays with her. Mother resisted, not wanting to be around her "bossy" sister, then

My Aunt Edna Schneidt in 1983.

agreed to give it a try for a short while. In the meantime George called to tell us he was passing through town en route to visit Eileen's family in Michigan. He wanted to stop in and visit with Mother.

I tried to dissuade him from bringing Eileen (who must have gotten over her anger with him) along on the visit. Mother was in a fragile condition at the time. She was on blood pressure medication, diuretics, and finally, an anti-depressant. The combination did not suit her well; she had diarrhea all the time.

The visit from George did not lift Mother out of her misery. Against my wishes, he brought Eileen with him on the visit. Mother sat and cried the entire time, until George got up and left.

A week later Aunt Edna called, sounding very concerned. "I don't know what is wrong with your mother," she said. "You had better come over. It's terrible."

Ron and I went right over. Mother was in the bathroom and Aunt Edna was sitting on a hamper right outside the bathroom door, with a bottle of Lysol in her hand, which she kept spraying the air with.

I went into the bathroom to help Mother. She was limp as a rag doll and started crying. "Oh, Katherine, what am I going to do? I'm all messed up."

"Honey," I told her, "there is only one thing to do. We'll get you cleaned up."

To Aunt Edna I said, "Please get us a clean gown, and quit spraying that damn Lysol."

We managed to get Mother cleaned up and in bed. I called the doctor, who suggested I bring her to his office in the morning for another checkup. He wasn't going to speculate on what might be wrong with her before running tests.

Once settled back in bed, Mother calmed down. I was speaking to her, trying to reassure her. She reached up and placed both her hands on my face. Then she gently pulled me down toward her and kissed me on one cheek and then the other, with tears in her eyes.

"What's wrong?" I asked.

"I'm so sorry," she said meekly.

"What are you sorry for?" I wanted to know.

"How I treated you all those years," she answered.

"Oh, Mother. Some of it I'm sure I deserved."

"No, you didn't," she insisted. "I always accused you of being like your daddy, and I really held it against you. But you are here and you have always been here for me. I pray God forgives me, and you will, too."

"Mom, there is nothing, absolutely nothing to forgive. I mean that from the bottom of my heart. Because it was a blessing to be your daughter and my daddy's daughter. Now, we are here together and that is all that matters. I'm going to sit right here until you get to sleep."

The next day Mother went into the hospital. As requested by Mother, I called George to inform him. He was back in town by then, staying with our son Danny. He couldn't accept that Mother had become all upset over his visit. "Oh, she'll get over it," was his response.

"No, George," I said to him, "this time I don't think she will. I can't explain it and I don't pretend to have knowledge why, but when you showed up with Eileen, it just totally shattered her heart."

"That is foolish. She has to get over it," is all he would say.

I told him, "If you want to see Mother one more time, you need to stop and see her at the hospital. But please leave your lady-friend downstairs."

So he went up to see Mother at the hospital and called from there to tell me.

"I'm sure she was glad to see you," I said.

"Yeah," he said. "And she was glad to see Eileen."

I almost gasped, "George, you didn't!"

"She's fine," he insisted. "It's your imagination."

I was back up at the hospital to see Mother again in the evening. "Are you okay?" I asked her.

"I am now, with you here," she said.

I assured her, "I'll stay as long as you need me."

"No," she protested. "You have to get home to your children. You have so much to do."

"No, I want to stay," I said. "And Ron is here, too."

Mother perked right up when she heard Ron was present. She loved Ron.

"And," I continued, "I have two kids out in the hallway. Do you want to see them?"

She perked up some more when they entered. But mostly she seemed like she had been given something to make her feel drowsy. The doctor on duty said she hadn't been given anything and didn't have a good explanation for her condition.

The next evening when I visited Mother in the hospital, I brought along my youngest, Georgia. We had a bouquet of flowers with us, and Georgia brought her fingernail polish, intending to fix up Mother's nails, something Mother used to love having done.

Mother was sitting up and, as we were visiting, suddenly she said, "Oh Katherine, look."

"What, Mother?" I asked.

"Don't you see it? It is the most beautiful stream I've ever seen. And look at those trees. They are gorgeous. They are in bloom. And look at those flowers along the shore."

Realizing what was occurring, I said to her, "Mother, you are getting a glimpse of heaven."

"Katherine," she continued. "It's so beautiful, and so peaceful."

The next morning I received a phone call from the hospital informing me Mother had not done well during the night. I took the children along and went right over to see her. She was in a half-conscious state, barely breathing.

I called the nurse in. Then the nurse asked me, "Is the doctor giving her something?"

Right then Mother started taking deep breaths, like she was gasping. The nurse turned to me, saying "I think you need to go. Leave the room."

As I got to the door I heard Mother take her last breath. I continued into the hallway and told the others she had passed away. Then I went back in and just held her. She looked like she was at peace. She looked beautiful. I couldn't help but say, "I know God's got her. Nobody can be dead and look so beautiful."

When a doctor came to examine her and pronounce her dead, I requested an autopsy. I knew my brother George was not going to believe she had died so quickly after he had convinced himself she was doing fine. As I told the doctor, "First, he is going to blame you, then he is going to blame me. So, to clear your name, get an autopsy done."

It took three days before we received an autopsy report. The certificate read, "No known cause of death." But in little print the results of tests were recorded. Next to "potassium" there was a zero. The doctors had not checked her potassium levels.

I've been a real tiger about potassium ever since, and I've seen a few other cases of people getting weak and finding out their potassium levels were low.

Our Cleaner Hands Formula, magical stuff that cleaned the toughest grease off hands and continued to heal them afterward.

Chapter Twenty

KATHERINE HARPER'S CLEANER HANDS FORMULA

One day I walked out to our plant and saw one of the men standing to one side, busy biting the side of his finger. I walked up to him and asked, "What's the matter?"

He put his hands out and said to me, "Mrs. Harper, look at my hands. I wish we had something that would clean our hands and not tear them up."

I wasn't unaware of the problem. Ron's hands used to get all dry and start cracking until they bled. It got to the point with Ron where I didn't even want him to touch me. If I wore a silk blouse or sweater, he could run his hands across it and just pick the heck out of it.

Many of the men were using industrial solvents to clean their hands. There was also some clay product they would wash their hands with, which would remove the grease and grime but leave their hands terribly dry. Clearly there was a need for a better hand cleaning product.

We had a chemist working for us at our Harper/Love plant who I really liked. I approached him and addressed him by name.

"Dick," I said, "I need a hand cleaner."

"Okay, Mrs. Harper. What kind of hand cleaner do you want?"

"One," I said, "that the guys can use and not tear their hands up in the process. Something that will actually help their hands."

He looked at me and said, "You know what you are asking for? You see these guys' hands?"

"Yes," I said, "I see them every day and I live with Ron."

"You are asking me for the impossible," he replied.

I had just finished reading a biography of Henry Ford. When Ford wanted something done, he would walk in and tell his engineers what he wanted.

And the engineers would say, "That is impossible."

Ford would then say, "I don't want to hear it. Just do it."

I tried that line out on Dick. "Just do it," I told him. "I don't know how you are going to do it but you will find a way to create this hand cleaner."

Four or five months later I saw him one day and asked him, "Where is my hand cleaner?"

"I'm working on it," he told me. "Just haven't got there yet. You know what you asked me to do?"

"Yes, Dick," I answered. "I have faith in you. I know you can do it."

About a month later he came in with a little jar and said to me, "I think I got it."

I was ready to put the hand cleaner to work right then and there, but he said he needed one more ingredient. He was searching for some sort of little scrubbing beads he could add to the solution to assist the cleaning process.

Our son Chris went to work with him at that point and they came up with something suitable. Then Dick produced enough of the hand cleaner to fill a fifty-five gallon drum. He told me, "This stuff is going to be tough to make. The competition isn't going to easily replicate it."

He explained how he had to take the ingredients through two different processes, one to mix two separate solutions, and a second to combine the two together.

We put a gallon jug of our new hand cleaner in the shop area and told the men they could try it if they wanted. Some preferred to stick with what they had been using. Others were game to give it a try.

After about a week one fellow said to me, "What in the heck is that stuff?"

I had to ask, "Why, what's wrong?"

"My hands haven't been this clean ever, and they aren't torn up," he said. "They are looking better than they have in a long time."

The men who used the new cleaner had remarkably better-looking hands after a week or two than those who didn't use it.

Ron came up with the idea of calling the new product "Katherine Harper's Cleaner Hands Formula." I never did like having my name on the product, but that is the way it was. The cleaner, a viscous liquid, was put into gallon bottles and assorted other sizes, and a photo of me appeared on the side of the label.

Katherine Harper Ltd

A SUBSIDIARY OF THE HARPER COMPANIES INTERNATIONA

We offered Cleaner Hands in a variety of containers.

Ron must have passed some of the hand cleaner on to our good friend Humpy Wheeler, who manages the motor speedway just northeast of Charlotte. Humpy called a few weeks later and told us, "You ought to bring this into NASCAR. You could really sell this stuff." He thought it was the best hand cleaner he had ever used.

Well, Ron is always looking for imaginative ways to do marketing. So we got ourselves involved in NASCAR racing. This was back in 1986. Nobody explained clearly to us how much it was going to cost. We were put in touch with a company that had a car and was looking for a sponsor. Being new to the sport, we didn't have a first-rate driver, or even a first-rate mechanic. But we splashed our product name all over the car and got ready for the races.

The first big race we went to was in Atlanta. It rained all day the day before the race. We drove out to the racetrack and to the VIP parking provided for us in a grassy area. When I got out of the car and stepped onto the grass, my high heels sunk all the way in. I couldn't move.

I called to Ron, "You have to help me. I can't get loose to walk."

To myself I was saying, "Oh Lord, what are we doing here? What are we doing here?"

But it was fun. I learned a lot about racing and automotive mechanics. We became acquainted with many of the drivers, which I really enjoyed. They knew about our Cleaner Hands product and some of them would say to me, "My wife absolutely loves you. I can touch her now and she doesn't scream."

I even received letters from some of the wives, thanking me. They also said they would use the cleaner to dab on stains on clothes before they put them in the wash, with incredible results.

We knew one fellow with hair as thick and stiff as a brush. He also had a serious case of dandruff. He picked up a couple of sample bottles of Cleaner Hands from us one day, intending on trying to interest his company in buying the stuff. He was on the road and had to travel four or five days before returning home. During his trip he ran out of his medicated shampoo, so he tried using Cleaner Hands on his scalp. He called us, all excited, a few days later.

"You won't believe what I am about to tell you," he said. "This stuff is fantastic."

After a few days of use his difficult dandruff problem was cured. He was so excited and wanted to know how he could get more, though he did acknowledge it took a little doing to wash all the little scrubbing beads out of his hair.

I had a surgeon call me and tell me I had to get the stuff approved.

"For what?" I asked.

"It's the only cleaning product I've ever found that will take off the red markings we use when preparing for surgery. It takes the ink right off. But to get it approved, you'll have to add some kind of antiseptic to the mix."

We knew people in beauty shops who used it. Customers would massage their feet with it.

Not that our NASCAR marketing venture was all that successful, though it was fun while it lasted. We didn't go to all the races. Jimmy and Chris traveled up to the Northeast to watch the races up there. Ron and I went to the races in Atlanta, Rockingham and Charlotte. I used to be scared to death someone was going to crash and get hurt. It bothered me to find out a lot of people go to races hoping there will be wrecks to liven up the action.

Our little car, #49, didn't do so well. We were watching a race at home on TV one afternoon when our car started smoking. The television camera zoomed in and started following the car to see what was happening.

Ron said afterward, "Dag gone, we're going to have to have a smoke bomb for every race. That was the only time—when there was something wrong with our car—that we ever got good TV exposure."

We didn't do so well in NASCAR, and in the end our Cleaner Hands formula didn't sell as well as we had hoped. Near the end of that first season we attended a big show at the old convention center in Charlotte. A bunch of the leading cars in NASCAR were being featured. I walked up to one of the exhibits and struck up a conversation with the people there, telling them, "We're involved in a small way compared to what y'all are, but I'd be interested in

Our Cleaner Hands Formula NASCAR. Watching the races, I used to be scared to death that someone was going to crash and get hurt, 1986.
Photo © Chobat's Historical Racing Moments, LLC by CMG Worldwide/ www.Chobat.com

knowing what it takes to get a good car and a good driver, so one can really compete in the sport."

"About $8 million," I was told.

"'Bye. See ya," I replied.

And to Ron I said, "This is not the business we are in."

It was probably the most expensive education we ever received.

As for the cleaner, I still think the stuff is a magic formula. But we never did market it effectively. And we quickly learned there is a lot of competition in the hand cleaner market. We would check in stores carrying our product and find that competing distributors were removing the bar codes on the shelves for our product so the supplies were not being replenished.

Here I am presenting a check to NASCAR outside pole winner Harry Gant on behalf of Cleaner Hands Formula, 1986. *(Photo courtesy of Dorsey Patrick, Lake Wylie, S.C.).*

I suppose we didn't focus on it enough. The product never gained momentum. I think a big mistake was attaching my name to it. We weren't selling a home cleaning product. We were marketing to mechanics and such. I can say one thing however: I never once got a complaint about that product. We just didn't know how to effectively market the product and didn't have the network of retail outlets to build a market for it.

Chapter Twenty-One

I'VE GOT TO KNOW WHO I AM

"Tell me who you are. Tell me who Katherine Harper really is."
The year was 1981. My questioner was a man by the name of Dr. Peter Miller, who ran the Hilton Head Health Institute, in South Carolina, offering month-long "boot camp" programs to people going through crises in their lives, or people who just wanted to shake their lives up some in order to get a new start.

I wasn't sure how to respond to his question and finally asked, "What do you mean?"

"Tell me who you think you are," he asked again, in a kind, reassuring voice.

Still, I didn't know how to answer. "I'm really not sure what you mean," is all I could think to say.

"Well, let me get you started," he suggested. "You are Ron Harper's wife?"

"Oh, okay, I'm Ron Harper's wife."

"You have children?" he continued.

"Yes, I am the mother of five children."

The questioning continued in an unthreatening, casual manner. My answers were simple and straightforward. I was my mother's daughter, my father's daughter, the sister of two brothers, niece to my Aunt Edna.

Dr. Miller began to detect how I defined myself according to my relationships with other people, particularly close family members. He wanted to know more about how I viewed relationships with others. But then he came back again to the same question, "But who is Katherine Harper?"

I sat there and thought for awhile, then told him I wasn't sure. I really wasn't sure.

Much had been happening in my life leading up to that point, and I hadn't been coping with the challenges very well. I was up to almost 170 pounds and pushing out of a size sixteen, which upset me more than anything. Women in my family have been heavy, and I didn't want to go there. However, the stresses of life were getting to me.

Ron and I have had a wonderful marriage over the past fifty-some years, but it hasn't been perfect. We've gone through some rough periods. What has made it even more difficult is that I really do think Ron has been a terrific husband. I don't want to be misinterpreted in this regard. He has been a wonderful mentor, encouraging me to do so many things I might not otherwise have done. Nonetheless, living with a successful, hardworking person can be difficult. Ron was constantly on the go. Five or six in the morning until nine, ten, even eleven at night. He may not have thought of himself as being stressed out, but just being around him could stress me out.

I know from my own experience how much effort it takes to build up a successful business. Part of me wants to admire Ron for his ambitiousness and drive, and I do. I think he is an incredible person. Still, there were times I longed for calm, peaceful moments alone with him, uninterrupted by phone calls and business meetings, and unaccompanied by clients or even friends. I needed him to be present for me, not thinking about tomorrow or his next business move, just being with me. I wasn't getting enough emotional connectedness.

In the meantime we had built a new home for ourselves, the large beautiful home we have enjoyed living in for the past twenty-five years. I actually visualized the house before there were any house plans, creatively coming up with the layout and designs I wanted. Ron was the one who wanted to go ahead and have it built. I guess he was eager to enjoy some of the fruits of his labor. But the mortgage we assumed on the house frightened me. Coming on top of money we had borrowed for our business, it raised my anxiety level. Ron would always say, "Things will work out," or "Didn't I tell you it would work out?" But I was the

The pool in the backyard of our current home, 1983.

one who handled the financial end of things and paid the bills. I was the one who had to keep tabs on the bank accounts each month and make sure we were staying solvent. The anxieties grew with each additional indebtedness we took on.

And there was more piling up in my life. My kids were grown and gone from home, leaving me with an empty nest. I had the hardest time when my mother died. I was still grieving her loss and ruminating about the way she felt betrayed by my brother George. Earlier, during the winter, I had been diagnosed with pneumonia and had to take a course of treatment. In addition, my monthly period was becoming more and more of an ordeal. One day I was down at the beach with friends when I suddenly started to hemorrhage really badly. My friends bundled me up and got me home, where I went straight to my doctor.

There were concerns over whether I might have cancer or something. As it turned out, I didn't have cancer, but my doctor recognized I was slowly melting down and needing a break.

When I heard of the Hilton Head Health Institute, it sounded like just what I needed. There was a twenty-eight day program, billed as a class act boot camp, aimed at helping people lose weight and get their lives back together. I was ready for it.

When I broached the topic with my Aunt Edna, she thought the idea was horrible. "I can't believe you are going to an institute. Something wrong with your head?"

"Well, it might be that something is wrong with my head," I told her. "But actually it is my whole body."

There were twenty-three people in the program I enrolled in at the Health Institute. Two of them were men. Weight control was an issue for just about everyone and a primary focus in the course. We all weighed in at the beginning and went on a strict diet. We took classes every day, discussing every aspect of life. I learned a lot about metabolism and diet. There was also plenty of assigned exercise, which we participated in together. I remember the men thinking they didn't need to do everything the women did, but in the end they did participate.

One good part about the program was the way the topic of weight loss was avoided. We never talked about weight. We did weigh ourselves every week, but we talked about losing inches and doing exercises to take the bad inches away while keeping the important inches. With exercise, one gains muscle fiber, which weighs more than fat cells do. So one's weight may not drop dramatically at first, even though one is losing fat. And muscle cells burn more calories than fat does, which further increases good metabolism.

The dieting was tough and the exercise was sometimes strenuous, while the classes we took were inspiring. We learned a whole new psychology regarding healthy living. Dr. Miller was also the first one to get me started taking vitamins. I had brought along my medical records for him to examine and base his recommendations on. In addition to all the learning, the group dynamics among the participants were terrific. We really bonded with each other.

We were nearly three weeks into the program when I had my one-on-one "who-are-you?" exchange with Dr. Miller. The exchange took place on a Thursday. Those of us in the program were looking forward to the weekend. This was going to be our first "leave" since entering the program and we'd planned some fun activities in Charleston.

But there had been other things on my mind as well. Ron had planned a trip to Mexico, together with some friends of ours. We'd been down there a couple years earlier and he wanted to do something similar again. He had already purchased the plane tickets and made reservations. Everything was in place for when I finished my boot camp experience. We were supposed to take off and go to Mexico.

Everything was in place except one thing: I didn't want to go to Mexico, no matter how great the resort was down there. It seemed every time we went somewhere special we took friends along, or business clients. I wanted to go somewhere where it would be just Ron and I together, where I would have his undivided attention, where I would have him all to myself. I didn't want to go to Mexico, even if the plane tickets had already been bought.

It didn't take Dr. Miller long to get me to confess what was on my mind. I told him about my dilemma, how I really didn't want to go to Mexico and go along with Ron's plan to spend another vacation with friends.

"Okay," he said, "What does Katherine Harper want to do?"

I didn't have a ready answer. I didn't know. I didn't want to disappoint Ron. I didn't want to have to tell him I didn't want to go. I didn't know how to tell him what I was really thinking and feeling.

Dr. Miller could see I had some work to do. He suggested I skip the weekend activities that had been planned with the other participants in the program, the trip to Charleston and all, which I had been looking forward to. "I want you to spend Friday, Saturday and Sunday working on this by yourself. Spend as much time alone as you possibly can."

I looked at him a bit flabbergasted and said, "Dr. Miller, that isn't fair. This is the first weekend we have had leave and we have plans to go to Charleston and…"

"How important is it to you to resolve this conflict?" he asked.

"Oh, it's really important," I realized.

"Important enough to do what I am asking you to do?"

I agreed. But he wanted me to do one more thing. He wanted me to get up in front of the group after dinner and tell everyone why I would not be able to accompany them to Charleston and enjoy the weekend with them. "Tell them you have one of the most important decisions you ever made in your life to make by Sunday, and you need the weekend to ponder the issues involved."

After dinner we had a brief session where some of the others talked about what they looked forward to doing over the weekend. Then Dr. Miller called on me to tell the group what was on my mind and what I planned to do. I told them about my dilemma, whether to go to Mexico or not. "Everything inside of me is saying no, don't go, I don't want to go. But I am afraid not to go because this is something Ron wants to do. However, Dr. Miller has asked me to…"

"No, no, no!" Dr. Miller interrupted me. "I only asked you what you think you need to do. You are not doing this because I told you to. Get out of this what-you-think-somebody-else-wants-you-to-do way of thinking. You have got to do this for yourself or it is not going to work."

"So," I continued, "while I love all of you and love being with you, I can't be with you this weekend. I can't go to Charleston and do all the other things we planned to do together."

"Well," everyone wanted to know, "what are you going to do?"

"Well," I told them, "I may be seeing you in passing when we get up in the morning, or if you are out walking along the beach, but mostly I'm going to be spending the weekend alone. I don't think I have ever spent three days virtually alone with myself in my whole life. But I know I have got to know who I am and where I want to be."

Later in the evening I telephoned our daughter Margie and told her what I was going to be doing. I also asked her to get on the phone in the morning and call our travel agency. "Find out about the availability of cruises to the Caribbean. I'll call you on Monday. Let me know what you find out."

For the next three days I mostly walked the beach. I must have walked at least fifteen miles a day. I was so full of energy the walking was easy for me. I felt like I was just floating along. Before I couldn't walk a mile in twenty minutes; now I was striding briskly at a fifteen-minute-mile pace.

Along the way I took breaks, sitting in the sand and contemplating my life. I read Richard Bach's book Jonathan Livingston Seagull, which I really loved. I gazed out at the ocean, watched the whitecaps breaking, and fixed my eyes on the distant horizon. There was so much more out there that I wasn't seeing.

By Saturday afternoon a transformation had begun to occur in me. I had spent the morning walking way up the beach. The sky turned dark with a heavy overcast. I turned around and started back, expecting to get rained on.

Suddenly, it was almost like I had wings. I started running. Then the cloud cover parted and this most beautiful, golden light came shining down on me as I ran along the beach. I felt like at any moment I was going to take off and start flying. I just kept running and running, full of energy and excitement.

When I got back to my room at the institute, I knew exactly where I was going, who I was, and what I was going to do. I called Margie on the phone and asked her, "Honey, did you check on the cruise?"

"Yes, Momma," she replied and gave me the details.

"Call the travel agent back and book it for two," I said.

"But Mom, what if Daddy doesn't want to go? Y'all were supposed to go to Mexico for two weeks."

"Book it for two, now. If he doesn't want to go, you pack your bags. You're going with me."

The next day, Sunday morning, I woke up early. I was dazzled by the incredible early morning light in the room. I looked around and felt elated. For the first time in years I had no desire for a cigarette. I walked over to the closet and pulled out the two cartons of cigarettes I had in there. I tore all the cigarettes up and threw them in the trash can. Then I thought to myself, "Okay, I'm getting to where I need to be."

Again, I spent the day walking the beach, but I was no longer questioning who I was or what I needed to do. I had gained a new confidence. I had a better grip on who Katherine Harper was.

Sunday evening the group was back together, with everyone reporting on the weekend's activities. When my turn came I stood up in front. My weekend had been different, and all the others were eager to hear what I had decided.

"I'm not going to Mexico," I started. "I'm not going to be at someone else's beck and call. I'm not going to do what somebody else expects me to do. From now on I am going to be who I really am and do what I really want to do."

Everyone stood up and applauded.

"Now, let's see how well I can handle all of this," I added.

During the final week of our boot camp, I went out and bought new clothes. I had to. I had gone from a size sixteen to a size ten. On my weekend alone I had struggled with whether to spend money on clothes and decided I wanted to. I went out and bought myself new shorts, slacks, sweats, the whole thing. I was feeling really good about myself.

We had a graduation coming up and I was hoping Ron would come to see me graduate. I wanted to surprise him with the new me. But he was scheduled to be out of town on a business trip, and he was expecting me to be back when he arrived home and be ready to take off to Mexico.

I talked with Margie, asking her if she would fly down with her husband, Hal, and son, Lee, and attend my graduation, then they could ride back with me in my car to Charlotte.

Ron called a little bit later. "I was talking to Margie to tell her to be sure to take the airline tickets to you when she comes down to your graduation," he started to explain, "and all she would say was, 'Dad, I think you better talk to Mom.' I asked her 'What about?' and all she would say was, 'You need to talk to Mom.' You've got to come. I've already bought the airline tickets. Don't you want to go?"

I took a deep breath. "No, I do not want to go to Mexico. I don't think I ever want to go to Mexico again unless it is just you and me on vacation by ourselves. In fact, what I have done is booked you and me on a cruise for next week."

There was dead silence.

"Are you there?" I finally inquired.

"Yeah," he said. "I hear you. You sure you're not coming?"

"I am absolutely certain. I'm sorry, Sweetheart, but I am not coming to Mexico. Now, if you don't want to go on this cruise with me, Margie is going with me. But that is your choice. You do what you want to do."

"You are not being rational," he replied.

"Honey, I am more rational now than I have been in as long as I can remember, for the first time in our married life."

"What if I call you back later and talk to you," he concluded.

Margie arrived for my graduation and could not believe it when she saw me.

"What do you think, Honey?" I asked her.

"Daddy is not going to know you," she said.

We drove back to Charlotte the next day. I needed to do a little more shopping and asked Margie if she had everything she needed for the cruise, because Ron still hadn't said whether he was going with me.

The phone rang as we were getting ready to go out. Margie answered it. Ron was calling to tell us when he would be flying in and to arrange for us to pick him up at the airport.

There was time for me to go out clothes shopping again. While in the program I had learned all about color coding and had myself color-coded to learn what clothing colors work best for me. Just about everything I had been wearing was wrong. Even my clothes had been draining me. So I took my swatches with me and bought a few outfits which were the right colors. I also had my face and hair done, got myself all fixed up.

Margie had come up with a plan for meeting Ron at the airport. She and Lee would go down to the gate to meet Ron. (This was back when people could go to the gate to greet arriving passengers.) I would hang back about thirty feet.

We followed the plan. Ron came off the plane and greeted Margie and Lee. Then they started walking towards me and passed right by. Margie started laughing. Ron asked her what she was laughing about.

She said, "Daddy, turn around and look. Momma is here. We just passed her."

He turned around and looked, then blurted out, "Oh my God, Katherine?" He was so amazed.

I said to him, "What you see now is what you get."

"Do I detect something else going on?" he asked.

Taking cruises was one of the few ways I could get Ron to leave his work behind and relax at bit. Here we are in 1985. (above)

Ron and I during a trip to Australia in 1983. (right)

"Yes," I answered. "I'm not going to be your go-for girl anymore. We are going to be true partners in what we do from here on in."

I don't think he fully understood me. He did agree to accompany me on the cruise, however.

We left for our cruise the next day and for the first few days we were strangers to each other. We talked to each other but we weren't communicating. I told him I was going to be happy with or without him. My preference, by far, was to be happy with him. But I was going to find a way to be happy no matter what.

Slowly, over the course of the week, we became reacquainted with each other. We could see how over the years we had changed. He had changed and I had changed. We have to adapt to change. In the month leading up to our first cruise together, I had become much more independent. But I could still appreciate being loved and affirmed by the husband I married nearly thirty years earlier.

We took part in a ceremonial renewal of our wedding vows aboard a cruise ship *(courtesy of Norwegian Caribbean Lines).*

Chapter Twenty-Two

KATHERINE HARPER FOR U.S. SENATE

The prompting that led to my candidacy for a seat in the United States Senate came to me in the middle of the night late in 1985. Up until then I had had no inclination to run for political office. Perhaps it was a dream, but to me it came across like a voice from atop a mountain—not an echo, but a strong, resounding revelation: "Run for the U.S. Senate."

I sat straight up in bed and said, "Ron, did you hear that? Ron!"

"Hear what?" he responded, groggily.

"That voice," I said.

"No. Go back to sleep. You were dreaming."

"No," I insisted. "This woke me up."

"Okay," he conceded, "we'll talk about it in the morning."

The next morning he broached the subject first. "What was that all about last night?"

"It was a strong voice," I told him, "that said, 'You must run for the U.S. Senate and disassociate yourself from your business.'"

Well, Ron wasn't too sure at first, and neither were some of our close friends in the political world when we told them. Some of them thought I was joking. But I was serious. I felt I had a message that needed to get out. There was a reason I had been commanded to run for U.S. Senate. What's more, I felt qualified to mount a campaign for the May 1986 primary election to be the Democratic Party candidate in North Carolina.

At a fundraiser with Doris Comartie, who initiated us into the world of Democratic Party politics in North Carolina, 1984.

Ron and I had become deeply involved in politics in North Carolina a number of years earlier. We started, quite innocently, by taking a course in the evenings at Queens College, in Charlotte, on the new Equal Employment Opportunity Commission (EEOC) rules, something we needed to be more familiar with for our business. The course was taught by a woman named Doris Comartie, who was active in Democratic Party politics in North Carolina and someone who became a dear friend.

We weren't actually looking to get involved in politics, but we asked Doris about ways we could become better known throughout the state for the sake of a new business venture of ours. We had recently acquired a heating and air-conditioning business and we needed to start doing some aggressive marketing to make it profitable. When Doris suggested political involvement as a way to network, we were a bit taken aback.

"You're kidding?" was our initial response.

"No, I'm serious," she told us.

It wasn't long afterward that we took a trip to Raleigh, and Doris introduced us to Governor Jim Hunt, Lieutenant Governor Bob Jordon, and a host of other state and national politicians. Soon we were up to our necks in political activities. Ron took on the responsibilities of state finance chair for Eddie Knox, the mayor of Charlotte at the time, who was running for governor. Jim Hunt was running for U.S. Senate after serving as governor for four years, and I became the Mecklenburg County finance chair for his campaign.

Our lives became more than a bit hectic during the campaign season. We spent a lot of time on the road to and from Raleigh. I felt like we were on a rubber band, springing back and forth nearly every week, and wished we had had the good roads we have today. Back then it took three-and-a-half to four hours to get there. Our weekends were crowded with political activities, including fundraising dinners at our home.

As the campaign heated up we became dismayed at how nasty politics can be. I had no idea how dirty it can get. Most of what we witnessed came from the Republican side, particularly the Jesse Helms camp. He was running against Jim Hunt for the Senate seat. The part I remember most was a story concocted by a little newspaper in the eastern part of the state that intimated that Jim Hunt was a homosexual. They even had a photograph, as I recall, showing Jim standing next to some guy he had never met before, with the accompanying story implying these two were lovers. It just went on and on. I could not believe it.

In the end both Jim Hunt and Eddie Knox lost their respective races. We started getting phone calls from people saying, "Please, don't get discouraged and quit. It's the first time y'all have been involved and we know losing can be hard to take."

People thought we would just say "to hell with it" and not want to have any part of politics again. But I think we had become incensed enough to not want to give up. It is nice to know everyone is human, but some can be subhuman as well. I remember asking Jim Hunt after the race, "Why are people lying like this? Why do they do this? And how do they get away with it?"

He just shook his head. He had done a lot for this state as governor and would have been a great senator. All he could say was "I don't know."

I suppose there have been times when Democrats have become nasty as well, though I never saw it in this part of the country. But the Republicans, it amazed me what they were willing to stoop to. And people were so quick to believe the rumors and innuendos. They would tell us, "Well, if you hear it often enough, it must be true."

Given all the sleaze I saw during that campaign season, there was no thought in my mind of running for political office myself. But I had begun developing plenty of ideas about what was needed. A friend once told me, "Governor Martin is appointing these businesspeople to positions of influence up there in Raleigh, people who were formerly CEOs of big companies."

That got my interest. I wanted to hear more.

He went on, "They're used to saying something and getting it done."

I liked hearing that.

"But," he went on, "that's not going to work up there."

"Why not?" I inquired.

"Because," he said, "government is not that way."

"Well," I said, "It is time for it to be that way!"

As I said, I was not contemplating running for political office. Until, that is, a voice in the night turned me around. I announced my candidacy in January 1986. We bought a Winnebago RV and painted "Katherine Harper for U.S. Senate" on it. Over the next few months I put in 16,000 miles crisscrossing North Carolina, pitching my ideas on what I thought was needed. We spent long weekends on the road, Thursday through Saturday, or Friday through Sunday. Ron drove the Winnebago some of the time. Danny would do the driving other weekends. It was one of the most fantastic learning experiences I ever had in life.

The public speaking skills I had learned in the Dale Carnegie course and honed further in a Ty Boyd Public Speaking Seminar came in handy. I had no problem standing up in front of large crowds in numerous settings and laying out my platform. I never wrote out my speeches, though we wished later we had recorded some of them. I never felt bound to a script and felt free to address personally, yet forcefully, each audience I encountered.

Some of what I advocated was what I had learned from my parents. The Democratic Party was the party of immigrants. I remember my father getting passionate about Democratic candidates running for office. In those days the party stood for opportunity. People weren't looking for handouts; but like my father, they loved America because America was the land of opportunity. These were people who had experienced oppression in the Old World and looked on the Statue of Liberty as a symbol of hope for a new beginning in a land of opportunity. No matter what station in life they found themselves in, they felt they could carve out a niche in this country if they were willing to put in the effort. What they wanted most was a chance to work and see their labor bring about betterment in their lives.

I had grown up in the period when, for twelve years, Franklin Roosevelt was president. He represented Democratic Party politics for many of us. We could remember how he stood up for the underdog during the long years of the Great Depression, opening up opportunities for people to earn a living. We could remember his fireside chats, how he assured us victory would be achieved during the terrible years of the Second World War.

The mid-eighties, when I was running, were the height of the Ronald Reagan years. I could also appreciate much of what he had done for this country, even though he represented a resurgence for the Republican Party. I will always give Reagan credit for making people proud to be Americans again. He reunited the country after years of dejection and divisiveness following the Vietnam War.

Our son Danny had served in the U.S. Marines in Vietnam. When he came home he was told to not wear his uniform. Soldiers and marines were fighting over there, doing what they were ordered to do, then were coming home and having people spit at them and throw things at them if they wore their uniforms. Reagan restored a pride in American strength.

Reagan also took much of what used to be central to Democratic Party politics and made it the Republican platform, particularly when it came to promoting fair and effective business policies. Now, it is true he went too far in favoring large corporations, but what became central to my political platform was the need to get back to the basics of sound policies that promote the growth of businesses.

More than any other issue, the need for the Democratic Party to get back to its roots, to the basics of what makes for a sound economy, is a theme I hammered away on. What angered me most was how so many Democrats had adopted an anti-business rhetoric. They wanted to blame businesses for all the ills of America. They spoke as if workers were the ones who gave, while business owners were just takers. They often promoted policies that encouraged more people to become takers, looking for handouts from a more socialistic government. They were taking some of Franklin Roosevelt's programs meant for a period of crisis and turning them into central features of our political economy. As a successful businessperson, I could see the dire, long-term economic consequences of going in that direction.

I remember being at a meeting of Democratic operatives. This one fellow, who I generally had a lot of respect for, stood up and started haranguing "business," going on and on about how business treated labor and so on.

I finally just had to speak up. "Stop! Listen to what you are saying. I'm sick and tired of Democrats running down business. If there were no businesses in this country, there would be no manufacturing. How many jobs would be available? What you are talking about are large conglomerates, big multi-national corporations, businesses that lobby to get favorable trade policies and tax breaks. Many of them don't even pay any corporate taxes. But the average, small and medium-sized business is in a different ballpark. We've got to make this distinction clear. We're not against business. We are against large conglomerates working together with Republican politicians to create a monopolistic and unequal playing field."

Even the use of the term "big business" bothered me. People think of a small business as one that employs ten to fifteen people. The Small Business Administration lists businesses employing up to 400 people as small businesses, yet most people think of a company with over a hundred employees as part of "big business," the monster most Democrats wanted to disparage.

I became more and more impassioned about this issue as the campaign wore on. I spoke at a lot of college campuses to crowds of students. One day I addressed a large gathering at a community college in the eastern part of the state. Four or five of the other Democratic Party candidates were on the stage that day, each taking a turn at the podium. Most of them spoke about "big business" and how bad businesses were treating people.

While one of the other speakers was going on about the ills of the business world, I leaned over and asked the director of the school, "What do you teach at this college?"

"Trades. It's a trade school," he answered.

"Tell me, what trades?"

He started listing them off: accounting, business, applications, and others.

"Um," I murmured.

He looked at me and said, "Why are you asking?"

"In other words," I said, "you are teaching students how to get along in the business world of trades and whatever."

"Yeah," he replied. "But Mrs. Harper, what are you thinking about?"

"Well," I answered, "what I was going to talk about is quite different than what I now want to get up there and say."

I was the last speaker. The first thing I said to the students was, "Okay, first of all, how many of you are in your last year of school here?"

About 75 percent raised their hands.

I went on, "From what I've heard, all of you hope to go out and make a good living with what you have learned while going to school here."

Of course I got the response I wanted: "Yeah, man!"

Then I went on, "But I'm confused, really confused. Because I heard the other speakers before me talking about how bad businesses are."

"Oh yeah," came from the crowd.

"Okay, I got your point," I replied. "But does anybody here equate businesses with jobs?"

Dead silence.

"Come on," I said, preparing to drive my point home: "Businesses equal jobs."

Nobody said a thing.

"Somebody on this side," I continued, "tell me what you hope to do when you graduate from this school."

Nobody responded. But I could see them thinking. I knew they were trying to put one and one together and not come up with three.

I finally pointed to a young man and asked him, "Would you stand up, please? What are you studying here?"

He stood and said, "I'm getting my certificate in electronics for heating and air-conditioning."

"Good," I told him. "We need people in that field. What do you plan to do with your certificate?"

"I plan to use it," he said.

"How?" I asked him.

He stood there for a while before someone from the other side of the room answered for him, yelling out, "You hope to get a job, stupid."

I applauded. Everyone else just sat there looking at me.

"Come on," I said. "Business isn't bad. Businesses create jobs. You need jobs when you graduate. You will turn to businesses to find those jobs. Some of you will start your own businesses. My husband and I own a business that manufactures parts for printing presses. We ship our products all over the world. We hire skilled laborers. If we can't get the kind of skilled employees we need, we train them or send them off to school to get trained.

"Quit hitting on businesses. Businesses are not all bad. The average business in this country is called a small business, and most people who are employed in this country work for small or medium sized businesses. Don't hesitate to get involved with a business. Hopefully your education here will have ignited a spark in you that will take you past employment

for a
New Face . . .
Fresh Voice . . .
Different Image . . .
in Washington!

KATHERINE H. HARPER

Co-founder and President	— Harper Companies International
President	— Harper Corporation of America
President	— Katherine Harper, Ltd.
Secretary/Treasurer	— Harper/Love Adhesives Corporation
Secretary/Treasurer	— MSC Harper Distributing Corporation
Secretary/Treasurer	— Harper Machinery Corporation
Board of Directors	— Arrowood Association-Present
North Carolina Banking Commission	—1982 to 1985
	YWCA, Charlotte —1984

Biography

KATHERINE HARPER, a native North Carolinian, was born on August 23, 1933. Her father was a Greek immigrant; a determined young pioneer who ventured to America alone at age 16. Her m_____grandparents, under similar circumsta____ during spirit, ar___ Hungary and G___ instilled a deep KATHERINE's on to future ge___

Proud to b___ North Carolini___ wants to serve___ 52 year old, sh___ a wealth of kn___ an extremely ___ of five childre___ already serve___ munity, in po___ nationally a___

KATHE___ person who ___ and a differe___ U.S. Senat___

Quotes

"I worry about the erosion of our freedoms as guaranteed by our inspired forefathers when they penned the Constitution. We must forever guard that important document with our life."

"American business and the American worker, working side by side, in harmony, produced a formidable destructive force to the enemy in World War II. We can, in a similar fashion, accomplish so much more in peace."

"Conflicting peoples and countries must recognize that life on earth is short. Real unity of purpose during this short span in time for each generation, could create a world free from hunger and a world free from violence and strife."

"The real giants of our time were men and women who loved life, who took time to smell the roses, and who shared their love, their life and their roses with others."

Katherine H. Harper

KATHERINE HARPER's campaign for the United States Senate is going to be one of the most exciting and fulfilling campaigns in North Carolina history! We'd like you to get involved. Political experience is helpful but not required.

For more information: Telephone (704) 588-4621
or write
KATHERINE HARPER,
P.O. Box 11390,
Charlotte, NC 28220.
Your dollar contributions may be sent to the same address.
THANK YOU FOR CARING ABOUT NORTH CAROLINA!

Paid For By The Committee To Elect
Katherine Harper, United States Senate
Democrat

KATHERINE HARPER for United States Senate

I enjoyed campaigning and our team worked hard!

in some company, to where you will want to become an entrepreneur and start your own business.

"Now, is there anyone here who wants to stand up and keep talking more about how bad businesses are?"

One young student stood up and said, "Well, I think we ought to give Mrs. Harper a round of applause because she has given us some understanding, where the others were just talking."

I had a trickier time speaking to audiences made up of members of labor unions. Labor unions have long been strong supporters of Democratic Party candidates, and much of the anti-business rhetoric in the party grows out of this alliance. I had been warned early on if I went after the unions or the Federal Reserve, I wouldn't live to see the end of my campaign. Nonetheless, I was delighted when I was invited to speak to a large gathering of labor union members and leaders in Raleigh. Again, I was one of five senatorial candidates in the Democratic primary on the platform taking turns at the podium.

I made a number of things clear in my speech. For one, I addressed the new policies being introduced by the Equal Employment Opportunity Commission, suggesting that there was "much in common between what the EEOC was instituting in the way of enforcement of rules governing employment practices, as well as workers' benefits and protections, and what unions had been struggling to do to gain workers' rights. Unions and EEOC need to form a partnership in this common cause."

I got applauded.

But I went on, speaking my mind bluntly. Recognizing the current business climate in the country, I contended that it was not the time for divisive labor-management relations. Labor strikes would only bankrupt businesses already struggling to survive. There needs to be more negotiated settlements, I said, with both sides sitting down and discussing what was really best for the employees and the business owners or stockholders.

"Yes, if there are companies making excessive profits, then that is a different story. If employees are being mistreated, there is a time for action. But companies go through hard times and it is not in the interest of workers to kill off the companies that provide their livelihood. Quit taking such an adversarial role against companies. Companies can't afford to just automatically raise people's wages when times are tough. And when union members protect workers who don't contribute in the workplace, it adds a terrible burden to the well-being of a company. You can't run a business that way and expect it to prosper. What's more, you keep doing it and you are going to put the industries which are so vital to our economy out of business because someone else is going to come along willing to do it cheaper and maybe even do it better."

A friend of mine in attendance later said to me, "Out of the five candidates who spoke today, when it came down to the part about real life and common sense, you took the cake. They will never give you the labor union's endorsement, but you probably won some respect for speaking forthrightly about things they know to be true."

I had no idea how prophetic I was being. Labor unions were just starting to take hold in the Carolinas, a part of the country with a long, populist, anti-union climate. Many of the textile plants were being unionized. Celanese in Rock Hill, General Tire, Westinghouse, and Fruehauf in Charlotte, and a score of other companies were unionized. Less than twenty years later, many of those textile mills and other manufacturing plants were closing, overcome by foreign competition. I can't help but think unions contributed to the crippling of many local manufacturing businesses.

While campaigning I spoke out regarding the need for employees to have a greater awareness of what it costs a company to keep them employed. Even in our own company, I started asking workers how much money they made. Eight out of ten could only tell me what their take-home pay was. They had little idea how much the company contributes to their retirement fund, their health insurance plan, their social security, unemployment insurance and other benefits, to say nothing about having to deduct their local, state and federal taxes. When workers complain about low pay, they forget about how much companies are obligated to deduct from their pay, money that is not added to company profits.

"If I had a choice," I use to tell people, "I'd have a window where employees would come and pick up their pay in cash. Then each employee would have to go to the next window and pay his or her federal taxes, then go to the next window and pay state tax, then social security, and so on. Only then, I think, would most employees appreciate how much the companies they work for are actually paying them, and how much their labor and services are costing the company."

Not surprisingly, I was accused of being in the wrong party. People told me repeatedly that my views were more Republican than Democrat.

I'll admit my views were unique among the ten candidates who were running in the Democratic primary. But I insisted my views were in keeping with the roots of the Democratic Party and what it stands for. Yes, there was a time in the latter half of the 19th century and the early part of the 20th century when a monopolistic, sometimes called "robber-baron" capitalism prevailed. Labor unions were needed to win workers' rights to a living wage and greater safety in the workplaces. Democratic Party leaders led the way in enacting legislation that broke up monopolies. But that was a different era.

What I felt I had to offer, something sorely lacking in most of the other candidates, was a businessperson's perspective on what is needed for companies to thrive so they can provide secure jobs to people in contemporary society. Most of the other candidates just seemed to want to take the easy route, laying the blame at the feet of big business without offering any kind of workable solution. I kept emphasizing that the Democratic Party needed to get back to its roots, and those roots lay in helping people to succeed on an even playing field where businesses can grow.

A number of other issues were a part of my political platform. I had strong feelings, and still do, about the need for tax reform. Yes, Ronald Reagan did bring about a tax revolution in this country, but on this issue I didn't support his efforts. Huge cuts in federal taxes were accompanied by equally large cuts in appropriations to states, which were left scrambling to meet budget needs. People weren't paying attention to what was happening. In the end, state and local taxes climbed dramatically, and average wage earners and middle-class people ended up paying more taxes than before. The tax cut was a big tax switch.

More specifically, I made it one of my hobbyhorses to advocate a crackdown on tax evaders. Not just companies, but all kinds of people routinely find ways to declare unwarranted exemptions. Companies set up offshore offices to evade paying corporate taxes. There are just so many ways people get around paying taxes, some of them quasi-legal, others blatantly illegal. I really felt more could be done to police this situation and to make taxation more fair across the board.

On behalf of the average taxpayer, I advocated putting an end to the unconstitutional practice of requiring people to pay taxes on taxes. Yes, the amount one pays in federal taxes is not deducted from the amount one is taxed on when paying state taxes. And when one pays social security taxes, the calculations are again made on the gross amount. It amounts to taxes on taxes, something I feel is unconstitutional.

There were other elements in my political platform but these were the main ones, particularly the part about needing to bring a business perspective to economic policy in order to help businesses succeed, thus providing more employment for workers. I didn't think Democrats should surrender this point to the Republican Party.

As I feared, I didn't get far before having to contend with the kind of nasty political maneuvers for which I had developed such a disgust in past elections. Shortly after I announced my candidacy, three lawsuits were filed against us. Two of them I didn't learn about until later because Ron didn't want me to be distracted and he handled the matter. One involved the racecar we sponsored in the NASCAR circuit. All three of the suits were frivolous and were dismissed but still cost us attorney fees. Later when I looked more closely into the charges against us, it became clear to me that all three of these lawsuits were politically motivated, intended to scare me away from running.

Apart from the worlds of business and labor, I also felt I had an ability to connect with people. North Carolina has a lot of rural and small town folks. I'd travel down to the coast and tell audiences about my father having run a restaurant in Jacksonville. I'd talk about Ron and me meeting in Wilmington. I used to have an uncle who had a bar called Carolina Bar, on Carolina Beach. We used to go there when I was a kid growing up. I fell in love with the people living along the coast. I'd say, "I feel a part of me knows this area and the people who live here."

Equally rewarding for me was to travel to the mountains in western North Carolina. You don't really see the people of the mountains until you get into a political gathering or some festival that is being held. There was one festival Ron and I attended, along with our friend Alfred Glover, called a "ramp festival," held someplace that felt to us like it was as far west as a person can go in North Carolina and still be in civilization.

There are all kinds of stereotypes about the people living in the mountains of North Carolina, but until you get there, you just don't know what people who live there are like. I wanted to see and feel the atmosphere of the place for myself.

We kept asking ourselves, "Why is it called a ramp festival?" and "What brought about this large annual gathering?"

We arrived at a big park, with a band playing under a gazebo and people doing country dancing. But what we were most struck by was a heavy odor pervading the place. The closer we got to the activities going on, the worse it got. I remember Alfred saying, "God, it is about to make me sick."

I told him, "Well, maybe there is a paper mill around here somewhere." It was that kind of smell.

As we walked up closer to where food was being served, I asked someone, "What is ramp?"

"You're smelling it," I was told.

"But what is it, some kind of animal or what?"

"No," the fellow explained to me, "it is a vegetable that grows in the ground, and it stinks. If you eat it, your whole body stinks."

I looked over at the cooking food and said, "You're kidding."

He went on. "When you cook it, it is sort of like garlic. Not so strong anymore." Since then I've learned a ramp is a wild plant common in the Appalachian region, which some claim to be the "sweetest-tasting and the vilest-smelling vegetable in Mother Nature's bounty."

All I could think was, "We're here as part of a political campaign. What is the politically correct thing for me to do?"

Ron was smart. He asked for chicken and baked beans, which only had a little ramp mixed in with them. When I came through the line, someone filled my plate with ramp.

I looked up at Alfred and said, "I hope you are hungry."

"No," he said, "but I am taller than most people. When you get to the point you don't want anymore, I have an extra paper plate to put over the top of our unfinished meals. I can kind of hide it before dumping it."

That was one of the more humorous moments of the campaign for us. But the more we mingled with the people at that festival, the more I fell in love with them. They got me out on the dance floor and taught me how to clog. It didn't take me long to catch on. I loved it.

I loved how down to earth and solid the people were. The women wore flower dresses with no shape. The men wore coveralls. I got caught up watching them, thinking I could feel their hearts beat. I was absolutely amazed how they lived so independently, not worrying about the rest of the world, taking care of their own, requiring nothing from the government, only wanting to be left alone. "Just leave us alone." That was the notion that resounded most. "Let us educate our own kids like we've been doing for centuries. Leave us to manage our own affairs."

They did give me an opportunity to speak, which I gladly accepted. I stood up in front of them and just said what I felt. "You know, I feel the deep roots of people in this wonderful community. I get the feeling all of you have ancestors who have lived in these hills since before the Revolutionary War. You have family bonds that go back centuries. I've never felt the kind of pride of belonging to a community of people that I feel here today. It was people like you who yearned for freedom enough to defeat the British, and people like you who have persisted in maintaining the freedom you have to choose your own way of life. I can tell you I applaud you and I'll do what it takes to help you preserve your way of life."

One sees a lot when on the campaign trail and the learning experiences pile up. But that gathering at a ramp festival in the far west of North Carolina was one of the most poignant experiences for me.

I think I was good at connecting with people. I didn't try to BS them. I could feel proud of the people who make up this great state of ours. I remember one woman who told me, "We've never heard anybody talk politically like you talk. You talk like you have a lot of spirit in you."

"I hope so," I told her.

"Will you be hurt if you don't win?" she wanted to know.

"No," I could honestly say, "because meeting people like you has given me the chance to really get to know North Carolina. I've always been proud to be a North Carolinian, but I can't say I really knew North Carolina until getting out on the campaign trail and meeting so many wonderful people everywhere I have gone."

The primary election day came in May. Some people thought I would just fall to pieces if I didn't win. But I was so thrilled that I came in fifth out of the ten people in the race. I couldn't believe I had done so well. "Come on," I thought, "I was a nobody in this big state five months earlier and I did better than some seasoned politicians."

Looking over the polls afterward I could see, as I had anticipated, how I had done better in the rural areas, both in the East and the West, than in the urban centers in the middle of the state. There just wasn't enough time for me to gain name recognition and get my ideas out everywhere.

I was disappointed more women did not vote for me, but not totally surprised. Most women at the time still seemed to think that being a U.S. Senator was a man's job. An encounter I had in Asheville one morning typified many women's reaction to my candidacy. Danny was with me, doing the driving. We had the Winnebago parked in a RV campground one morning. I was standing outside the Winnebago waiting for Danny to get ready. A lady about my age walked up, looked at me and, motioning to the "Katherine Harper for U.S. Senate" painted on the side of the Winnebago asked, "Do you know who this person is?"

"Well, yes, I do," I responded.

"Well," she said, "I'd like to know what gives her the audacity to think that she can run for a position of this status."

I looked at her and said, "The same audacity it took you to ask your question in the first place. I'm Katherine Harper. Glad to meet you."

Terry Sanford won my endorsement in the 1986 senate race in North Carolina. He later invited us to a visit in his office in Washington, D.C. on several occasions. Pictured here from the left are our grandson Jason Harper, Ron and I, Senator Terry and Margaret Rose Sanford, and our grandson Lee Kluttz during one of our visits in 1990.

She turned and walked away, leaving me to think to myself, "Yeah, that's what I love, the female support." There wasn't much, even among party stalwarts.

Even before the campaign was over, I found another way to participate in the process. By then I had recognized in Terry Sanford the kind of leadership this state needed. He had served as governor and then been president of Duke University. I started telling audiences, "If you can't vote for me, vote for Terry Sanford."

Terry ended up winning the primary, and he asked for my help in the November election against the Republican candidate. I was more than happy to give him my endorsement and worked to see him get elected. While doing so we became good friends, both with him and his wonderful wife, Margaret Rose. They invited us to visit them several times after they were settled in Washington, D.C.

With the increasing influence of corporate lobbyists on our political process over the past twenty-five years, the political climate has changed dramatically in this country, and many politicians have become less attentive to the needs of people. It is easy to get discouraged and think there is nothing we can do about it. I used to address this feeling when I was campaigning. I'd tell people they can do more than just go to the polls and vote. What they need to do is get to know the candidates running, beyond what political party they represent. Really get to know what they stand for and what they are like, then put the word out about them. Shed some light on the issue. Talk about it. Don't be afraid to speak up in favor of candidates you feel have integrity and can best do the job.

After one campaign stop where I spoke about this matter of getting involved, a lady came up to me following my speech. She had to be eighty years old, cute as a button. She pointed her cane at me and said, "Honey, now you look at me. Tell me what I can do."

I just loved it. I asked her, "You have a telephone?"

"Oh yes, I got to have a telephone," she said.

"Well," I told her, "let me tell you a little story to illustrate what it is I want you to understand. I was in a church on Christmas Eve. They handed out little candles about three inches tall to everyone present. I had never seen this done before. Once all the candles were passed out, one person appeared with a lit candle and the ceiling lights were put out. Then the one person with a lit candle lit the candles of several people standing next to her. Then those people passed their flame on to others around them. Before long the room was almost as light as it was when the electric lights were on. The minister then asked everyone to hold his or her candle up high. 'See what one little candlelight can bring about,' he told us."

"Now," I told my rapt listener. "I want you to think of your telephone as a little candle. I want you to call and light as many candles with your telephone as you can. Call your friends and tell them to pass the word along. We've got to get involved and we've got to realize we can make a difference."

"Honey," she said to me, "I can't wait to get home to my telephone. I know I can get on it and light a lot of candles."

Chapter Twenty-Three

SPEAKING MY MIND

During the course of my life I have had plenty of experience in churches—the Catholic Church in particular, but different protestant denominations as well. Some of my experience has been good and helpful. I still have fond memories of my early years attending the Catholic Church, the mystery and the holiness I felt. But I've also been seriously disillusioned by much of what goes on in churches, particularly the human element in religion and how it can interfere with our relationship to the divine.

To me it was always natural to ask questions, and having learned different practices and doctrines from attending a variety of churches when I was young, I was always wanting to know how one God and one Bible could lead to so many different views. I always questioned "Why?"

Too often the response given to questioning in churches is an authoritative admonition to quit asking and just accept what is being taught. I could never go along with that. I wanted to understand what I believed. Nor could I accept that the opinion of a priest, or what a priest said needed to be done, was the last word on the matter at hand.

Ron and I have run into problems when we've been involved in fundraising efforts on behalf of charitable causes. Misappropriation of money sometimes occurs. We put in a lot of time and effort over the course of a couple of years in the mid 1960s raising money to provide updated library books for the Catholic school library by hosting fundraising dinner dances. When the priest decided much of the money could be better spent paving the parking lot, you bet we questioned him.

I have long wondered why churches don't do more to provide daycare centers. There shouldn't be a single child left alone anywhere. A parent should have somewhere to place her child and know the child will be cared for. While serving as president of the ladies guild at St. Patrick's Church, I finally found an institution offering the kind of love and support for children I had often envisioned, even going beyond my ideals. Holy Angels Nursery was managed by Sister Mary Patrice, who I had known from my school days. The nursery cared for dying babies. All the small children there had terminal conditions. Yet they were cared for so beautifully, dressed in pretty little outfits and changed regularly. All the cribs had brightly colored sheets. The love in the place was overwhelming.

I asked the Sister if she needed financial assistance. "Does the Catholic Church or any other organization raise money or contribute?"

B'nai B'rith did, but that was about it.

"Okay," I said, "now we know what our ladies guild project is going to be."

We put together a great plan involving a Christmas tree choir made up of students from the O'Donahue School. We would charge admission for the program and the money raised would go to assist Holy Angels Nursery. We made outfits for the kids and had dress rehearsals. Everyone involved was so excited, just ecstatic about what we were doing.

Somehow the priest got wind of what we were up to and he was in touch with me to tell me the money raised would not be going to Holy Angels Nursery. I don't know what his reasoning was, but he wanted control over the money raised, even if it was the ladies guild doing the fundraising.

By then we had flyers printed and the kids had been rehearsing and all. Nonetheless, I wasn't about to be involved in raising money for one stated purpose and have it go to something else. I told the others in the guild we would have to cancel the event if we couldn't donate the money to the nursery.

Others told me the priest responded by preaching a mini-sermon about me the next Sunday morning in church. A few weeks later he showed up at our ladies guild meeting, something he had never done before. The guild had grown quite popular under my leadership, up from about twenty members to sixty members. The priest came loaded for bear, with another mini-sermon on the authority structure in the church and where faithful parishioners are supposed to fit in. He started in on the duties and obligations parishioners have to the priests and nuns and kept going.

I had heard enough before he got very far. I stood up, looked at him, and said, "I want everyone in this room to listen to what I am saying. My first obligation in this world is to God. My second is to my husband and family. The third is to the Church."

Then I looked right at him and said, "You aren't even on the list."

Almost everyone in the room applauded, and I walked out.

I've found, in general, when faced with religious authority figures people are often afraid to speak up and defend what they believe. People are not used to questioning, to demanding better explanations, or even complaining about what may be a blatant misrepresentation of the truth. That hasn't been the case with me. No one can say I'm not an outspoken person.

There was an incident with Margie when she was in the first grade that has always stuck with me. When our kids were young, I used to take turns with another woman in the neighborhood carpooling our kids to and from school. One day as I was approaching the school there were a bunch of fire trucks all around. A half-block from the school a house had caught on fire. Black smoke was pouring out, and I watched as a fireman tried to enter through an attic window. I learned two small kids had been up in the attic. One, I later learned, was a classmate of Margie's. They were both home sick and had gone up into the attic and built a little altar on which they lit a couple of candles. Somehow, a candle must have upset and started the fire. Both children died of smoke inhalation before they could be reached.

When I picked the kids up at school the following day, Margie was in tears. What she told me when we arrived home was that the nun teaching her class had told the children the reason those children died was because they had disobeyed their parents and started a fire. "You see what will happen and what God will do to you when you disobey your parents," the nun told them.

I was furious and went right back over to have a talk with the principal. "It was bad enough that Margie lost a classmate," I told him, "but to say the whole reason the children died was because God was angry is horrible. That is not how God operates."

I don't think our children came away with a good impression of the Catholic Church. The unfortunate thing is they mostly remember the bad things about their Catholic school education and their years attending Church services and taking catechism classes and all. None of them married or even wanted to get married in the Church.

It is not just in Catholic circles. I grew up in Charlotte as a contemporary of Billy Graham, a native son of the Queen City. For the most part I have admired him for his ministry, but even with him I think there has been too much emphasis on hellfire and damnation. The reason Christ came was to show a softer side, to offer God's forgiveness. He taught that the centrality of the law of God was the law of love: love of God and love for neighbor.

I could go on and on about my grievances over the way religion is too often preached and practiced. In retrospect, I realize something essential to who I am has always been a willingness to question authority, especially when I see something wrong being done. I learned from dealing with my father how to stand up and speak my mind, even to an intimidating authority figure. But now I see a greater purpose for what I learned from the experience.

What has always given me the confidence to know when to speak up and what to challenge goes back to the spirituality I learned from my grandmother and the religious insights I cultivated as a young person. There was a foundation there, an experience of the holy, of the presence of the divine. When my grandmother would speak of "keeping God's presence," I think she understood something really, really important. There was enough of that experience in my early life for me to know

214

My brother George as chief of police in North Bay Village, Florida.

how to distinguish true godliness from human religiosity. I just have never liked it when the latter masquerades as the former.

In 2003 my brother died after a long decline into dementia. Near the end we found it difficult to communicate with him, though he still could remember Ron and me, and could even occasionally have moments of clear insight, with little bursts of light when he understood a conversation for two or three sentences. I tried repeatedly to get a priest to go see him.

George had a tough life, never having fully recovered from the post-traumatic stress disorder that resulted from his experiences during World War II. He never would tell us about what he had gone through in combat. His war-time marriage ended in divorce and it was sixteen years before the Church would grant him an annulment. He never did remarry and became indifferent to religion. He worked as a police officer down in Florida. Until near the end of his life, he continued to have a consuming hatred for our father.

Knowing his health was rapidly declining, I wanted a priest to speak with him, maybe take his confession, and give him some assurance and solace. There were some difficulties finding a priest willing to see him, but when I finally located one, I told him some about George and his life.

When the priest went to see George, he walked into the room, stood by his bed and said, "I hear you have a problem."

Even in his demented mental condition, that was not the kind of thing one said to George, or should say to anyone.

The priest told me afterward, "Your brother virtually threw me out of the room. I had to run to get away from him."

"You're lucky," I told him. "Why in God's name did you ever go in there and say 'I hear you have a problem'? Everyone in that healthcare facility has a problem. You weren't sent there to tell him he had a problem. You were sent there to give comfort."

Lest anyone think priests have always been the focus of my wrath, I'll add that there are priests who I believe are close to being saints. Before my brother passed away on August 23, 2003 (sadly, it was my birthday), another priest went to visit him, none other than Monsignor McClarin at St. Patrick's Cathedral. He telephoned me one day and introduced himself, then said, "I've been over to see your brother."

I was surprised and wanted to know why he would take the time go visit my brother. He'd heard about George's earlier, less-than-friendly, encounter with the priest who had visited the week before, and he told me he "felt the situation warranted his immediate attention."

I just started to cry. Simple acts of kindness like that are what keep me persuaded God's love can be present in people and be manifest through them. Why don't we see it more clearly? Why don't we make letting God's love show through us the biggest priority in our lives?

Eight days later my brother died. But during those eight days I saw a peace in him he had not had earlier. The Monsignor's visit, his compassion and counsel, had shown my brother the way to peace before he passed away.

Ever seeking to better understand spirituality on a deeper level, I have read so many books. My studies have not been confined to the Christian tradition. I've been richly inspired by reading the works of people like Yogananda, his *Autobiography of a Yogi*, and *The Second Coming: The Resurrection of the Christ Within You*. I've also read a lot of Edgar Cayce, someone who devoted his life to reminding people of spiritual resources not often sanctioned in our society.

I turned to these teachers to learn more about some of the things Grandmother told me about. She believed in reincarnation. She believed if a person committed a grievous sin in a former life, they needed to learn what it was in order to be able to "burn it off" in the form of a penance, making amends for what they had done. Learning about our past lives can therefore be important in order to expiate our past wrongs and keep us from repeating them.

There is also a belief that learning of our former existences can help us identify underlying purposes for our lives. Such purposes carry over from one life to the next, though people generally lose touch with their former selves. Reconnecting can give a person insight into what he or she is supposed to accomplish in this life.

I've come to learn that such notions were not uncommon in the early Christian tradition, but church authorities later tried to suppress them—though these ideas were kept alive clandestinely by people on the margins of societies. My grandmother must have learned about them from her Gypsy roots.

Grandmother also believed in a general connectedness of spiritual energy across time. Somehow she was attuned to a psychic energy that enabled her to see into the past and predict the future. The one that most amazed me is how she predicted my future, telling me "You can't imagine how successful you will be."

I have long been intrigued by these ideas, in no small part because I have had experiences myself which don't lend themselves to easy explanations. One day I was getting ready to attend a meeting. We employed a lady, named Ethel Choate, who did housework and ironing for us. I told her as I was leaving, "We are not expecting anyone and if the doorbell rings, just ignore it."

I left for work and was about halfway there when there was a voice telling me, "Go back to the house."

"What did I forget?" I started thinking.

I did go back to the house, and when I entered, Ethel asked me, "What did you forget?"

"I don't know," I told her, but I knew enough to follow the lead of the voice I had heard.

Pretty soon the doorbell rang. Ethel offered to get it, but I told her, "No, I'm on my way. I'll get it."

I looked out through the peephole in the door and didn't see anybody. Back then we didn't have a storm door, so I didn't want to open the door without knowing who was there. When I peered around from the window to the side of the door, I could see a man with his body up against the front door.

"What do you want?" I demanded.

"I ran out of gas," he said.

"Back up so I can see you," I said. "I don't have any gas. I don't keep gas on the property."

He started walking off, not turning to look at me. He had long hair and a beard.

"You better get out of here because I'm calling the police right now," I yelled at him.

What made me know I needed to go back to the house to deal with that situation? As Ethel said afterward, "I probably would have answered the door and been beaten to death."

Some people would say it was all a coincidence. I think much of what people attribute to coincidence may actually have more behind it. We just don't have the insight to be able to understand the interconnectedness of reality. I never thought it was coincidence when, just before the birth of our first baby, Ron was unexpectedly sent a check for three hundred dollars for extra duty he had performed in the Marine Corps. Ron thought it was coincidence. I knew better.

I have never believed the coming together of certain factors that were key to our success in business were just coincidental. The development of thermal flame spray technology and laser beam engraving gave us the competitive edge we needed to succeed. We may have had the creative insight to put everything together, but we had nothing to do with creating the juncture of those innovations at that point in history, just when we were getting started in business. I could give many more examples.

There have also been other times when I seemed to receive messages that gave me clear directions on what to do. When I first met Ron I just knew I was going to marry him. There was no doubt in my mind. Before I ran for U.S. Senate I had no intention of doing so, until, in the middle of the night, I received that clear directive to enter the race, even though I had never held a political office before.

My experience with psychics, other than my grandmother, who I consider to have had psychic powers, is rather limited. I actually would advise friends to be careful in seeking consultations with spiritual mediums, as there are a lot of charlatans out there. My own reservations about being swindled kept me from seeing any kind of medium for years. But the combination of a number of events finally brought me around to giving it a try.

We had a wind chime made out of seashells hanging in a doorway in our home. For about a month I kept hearing those chimes and began to notice how they often chimed when there wasn't any wind blowing. I began to suspect there was more to this phenomenon, as if I was receiving a message telling me someone was trying to contact me. Furthermore, I thought it might be my father. I began to think he may have graduated to some spiritual plane where he could now communicate with me.

About the same time, we had a friend who had invited a renowned spiritual medium from Washington, D.C., to her home. She spoke highly of him and told me she was lining up people to come and consult with him in her home. A bit reluctantly, yet intrigued by the sounds of the wind chime in our home, I agreed to see him.

At the start of the session he set up a cassette recorder, intending to record what was said. Somehow, I knew the recorder would fail to work and I told him so. He insisted it was his recorder and it was in good working order. We began the consultation.

He started out by telling me, "I know why you are here. You are getting signals from someone trying to contact you."

"Yes," I said.

"Do you know who it is?" he asked me.

"Yes," I replied, "I think I do. I'm pretty sure I know who it is."

"Who is it?" he asked.

"You're the psychic. You tell me," I told him.

"It's your father," he said. "He wants you to know how sorry he is for all the strife and conflict he caused in your life and in your mother's life. And he wants you to know he loves you dearly."

I began to get the smell of carnations and remembered how they were my father's favorite flower. I mentioned this, and the medium said my father's favorite color carnation was red. He was right. When Daddy would get all dressed up he used to like to have a red carnation for a boutonnière.

Our conversation continued for awhile. The medium correctly identified what line of work I was in and spoke of seeing water and land. We happened to be looking for property on Lake Wylie at the time to build a weekend home.

As our exchange was winding down, the medium looked at me and said, "Now it is time for me to ask you a question. You knew everything I told you, didn't you? You knew every single thing that I told you today."

"Yeah," I had to admit. "I have feelings."

"You are more psychic than I am," he told me. "Why aren't you letting it come through?"

Tears started rolling down my cheeks, huge tears.

I tried to explain, but couldn't get the words out. "The few times… I don't discuss it. I just react to it. I can't…"

Finally, he asked me to stand up. He wanted to give me a hug. Then he surprised me by disappointing me.

He said, "Honey, if you team up with me, we could make a fortune."

"No way," I said immediately. "It is God's gift, something I can't turn down. But it is a huge burden. I'm just in awe of what all is involved. Not that I know everything, by any means, but I can sense and feel things, and I react to things I experience."

We left it at that. And, as I predicted, the recording of our session turned out blank.

Another encounter I had a few years later with a psychic was more overwhelming for me and gave me an enormous amount of food for thought. I really don't know what to make of it all, whether to believe what I learned is true; but I must say, there is a lot of affinity between my life experience and what I "saw" during a past-life regression.

Ron and I took a vacation in Arizona at a beautiful spa. The place offered all sorts of amenities and activities, from exercising equipment to massages. There were a number of health specialists available to speak with. And there was a resident doctor who did past life regressions.

I had a fair amount of apprehension about seeing this doctor. I know past life regressions can be dangerous. There is no telling what will be revealed and how one will react to the material. So I asked for opinions from others who had been in consultation with him and received all kinds of assurances from them. People said he was tops in his field.

When I did go to see him, I asked that he not take me any place "where I can't hear your voice."

We discussed the matter for awhile, the seriousness of what is involved and all. He seemed very reassuring. Then he offered to "take me down."

I was lying on a futon, somewhat propped up on pillows. He took me down, saying, "Let's go back to the beginning."

I really had no great sensation to begin with. There were no special effects like one sees in movies. Nothing dramatic.

"What are you seeing?" the doctor asked me.

"It's dark, very dark," I said.

"Any light at all?" he asked.

"Oh wait, here it comes." I was seeing something emerging. "Now there is light and it is beautiful."

"Are you in the beginning, at the creation of the earth?" he inquired.

"Yes," I answered, because it really felt like it.

"Are you watching God in his creation?" he asked again.

"Yes, and it is gorgeous, just beautiful."

Then I heard him say, "Let's bring you forward."

All of a sudden I found myself standing on a hillside, on top of a huge rock. Down below the rock was teeming with people. They were all screaming.

The doctor asked, "What are you doing?"

I explained the scene to him and told him, "I'm screaming back at all the people."

"What are you screaming back at them?" he wanted to know.

I said, "I'm telling them the messiah is here."

"The messiah?" he questioned. "How are you dressed?"

I looked at my garments. "I'm dressed as I am supposed to be dressed. What do you mean?"

"Start with your shoes," he suggested. "Describe your shoes."

I looked down and could see I was wearing sandals. I had a robe on made of camel's hair.

"Why are you yelling at the people?" he wanted to know.

"Because they won't believe me. They have got to believe me," I exclaimed.

"And who is the messiah?" he asked.

"It is Jesus Christ," I answered. "He is coming, and I am here to protect the people."

My next awareness was of being brought back into the present. I was shaking, shaking like a leaf. I didn't know what to think of what I had just been through.

"I can't believe this," I said. "I don't know if I can walk out of here. Is this rigged or what?"

So he asked me, "You know where you were, do you not?"

I was still shaking some and in a state of disbelief. "I'm afraid to say," is all I could tell him.

I struggled for a long time afterward over what to make of my life regression experience. It was awhile before I even told Ron about it. I have never, before or since, experienced anything of that nature.

With my interest piqued, I read everything I could about John the Baptist in the Bible and other available sources. John was someone who asked a lot of questions. He wasn't afraid to question people in authority. He challenged authority figures who were not acting justly. And he got into a lot of trouble for his fearless questioning.

Whatever one thinks of reincarnation—and I'm not altogether sure myself—I do realize that on some level of consciousness my experience in the spa in Arizona was incredibly profound for me. Even if I understand my "past life" experience only metaphorically, what it made me aware of was how much I have been a John the Baptist-like figure during my life.

My mother used to tell me she didn't know where I got it from. She could only quietly envy my willingness to stand up to my abusive father. I could do so even after having witnessed my father kill a man in self-defense; even after having watched him repeatedly and violently beat my older brother; and having watched scenes where he verbally abused my mother, disparaging her in every way he could think of. Still, without the slightest fear, in full confidence that he wouldn't hurt me, I used to stand up to him and speak my mind. I didn't know where I got the courage from.

I can't help but think of all the times in Sunday school classes when I was the only one willing to ask the tough questions. I think of when I attended the Catholic school, how I didn't cower in the face of religious authority figures. Priests and nuns to me were people—fallible like the rest of us and needing to be corrected when they abused their authority. I didn't hesitate to speak up when I thought they were out of line.

Even in jobs I have held, I have often been the sole figure willing to speak up. My experience when working for the bank in Greenville, when I challenged the bank hierarchy with a long list of complaints and suggestions for improvements, was a case in point. I had a bit of trepidation that time, but in the face of warnings to keep my complaints to myself, I went ahead and said what I felt needed to be communicated.

Speaking my mind has been part of my nature. Whether it has been in my marriage, in our company, or when running for U.S. Senate, I have always been someone who is willing to speak up and make my views known. Maybe it is a carryover from a past life. But no matter what the source, it has been an important feature of who I am.

Whatever our connection on some cosmic plane, I have to say I've come to like the figure of John the Baptist. I admire him for his courage and his willingness to challenge those in power. Much of my admiration, no doubt, springs from a common nature. I can identify with him. All my life I've been like him.

There was more, however, to John the Baptist than his willingness to speak out and challenge those in power. When he stood before the teeming masses in the desert of Judea, dressed in a camel hair tunic and leather sandals, he proclaimed the coming of Jesus Christ, the manifestation of the love of God. He was known as the forerunner of Jesus, the one who prepared the way. When it comes to what is worth speaking up for and what really matters, is there anything more important in life? Isn't following his example what really matters in life?

Chapter Twenty-Four

WHAT REALLY MATTERS?

*A*ll too often we forget what really is important in life. We disregard the miracle of life itself. We neglect our relationships with those closest to us. We ignore our spiritual sources of meaning and values. I have had to learn, through times of crises and suffering, to re-examine my commitments and my priorities. I've learned much from my experiences.

I woke up in the middle of the night once back in 1982 feeling like someone had jabbed hot needles behind my jaw on the right side of my head. The excruciating pain came out of the blue, totally unexpected and without warning. I had gone to bed feeling healthy. Suddenly, this unbearable pain all but incapacitated me. I sat up straight in bed and then had to stay motionless to prevent another piercing round of agony from hitting me.

The pain finally subsided, and in the morning I went to see my dentist, thinking something must be wrong in my jaw. He diagnosed me as having an abscessed tooth. I hadn't been aware of any problems with my teeth but I was willing to believe him and let him pull one of my teeth—anything to avoid another round of what I had gone through during the middle of the night.

The dentist extracted a molar on the top right side. Having a tooth pulled can be an ordeal, but this was nothing compared to the earlier pain. It felt good to be rid of the offending tooth.

Ron accompanied me back out to our car afterward. As I was getting in, I got walloped again with the same pain, so forcefully I crumpled to the ground.

Ron came running around the car and helped me up. "That didn't do it?" he asked.

"Obviously not," I said, but I figured it was a matter of giving my jaw time to drain and clear out the offending infection.

We arrived home and as I was getting out of the car, it hit me again, like a bolt of lightning striking the side of my head. Then twice that night the pain struck. I was getting to where I was afraid to even breathe for fear the excruciating agony would strike again.

In the morning I couldn't wait to get to the dentist's office again. I called for an emergency appointment. The dentist I had seen wasn't in, but there was a female dentist available. I told her about the pain returning, and she said, "Oh, I was afraid of that."

"Afraid of what?" I demanded.

"That wasn't it," she said and suggested I go to see a specialist.

We arranged an appointment for that morning. By then I feared the pain would hit and knock me over anytime I moved around. But we went to the clinic we were referred to and checked in. When my name was called to go and consult with the doctor, Ron started helping me down the hallway. Again, in a flash, it was like hot needles stabbing into the side of my head. I just collapsed, with Ron keeping me from hitting the floor too hard.

The nurse called the doctor, who came out into the hallway. He said to me, "I want you to open your mouth and I hope the pain doesn't hit again, but I think I know what the problem is. It has nothing to do with your tooth, but I need to check where your tooth was pulled."

He looked at where the tooth came out and said, "Damn, that tooth was no more abscessed than I am invisible standing here. He should never have pulled your tooth."

I wanted to know what was wrong, and he went on to explain, saying, "I've seen only two other cases like this. You need to see Dr. Lassiter, a neurosurgeon. I'll speak to him and make some arrangements for you."

After making some phone calls he came back to explain the matter further to us. He suspected what was wrong with me—and it turned out to be right—was something called tic douloureux (also known as trigeminal neuralgia), a neurological complication involving nerves which affect facial muscles, in my case those that are splayed out just behind the jaw. He spoke of the nerves behind the jaw needing to float like a feather, and he said if the nerves get compressed by blood vessels or tension, the result can be the kind of excruciating pain I had been experiencing.

A CT scan was needed to confirm the diagnosis. I was hoping I wouldn't have to have one of those, but I got through it. It took a few days to get a definitive interpretation of the scan, and I was given painkillers to help me cope in the interim.

When the CT scan analysis came back, I met with Dr. Lassiter. He wanted to know what I had been up to, how life had been going for me. I told him things were pretty normal, meaning I was busy as ever. I had been very occupied in the company and we had been active in political fundraising, hosting events at our home and all. One thing would lead to another and I'd keep going, doing my best to keep everything running smoothly.

Then he explained how stress can build up behind the jaw, leading to neurological damage and tic douloureux symptoms. He recommended I try acupuncture to relax the area around the back of my jaw, and that I try to eliminate some of the stressors in my life.

"You are entirely too young to be getting these symptoms," he told me. (I wasn't even fifty yet.) "But whatever you are doing, I want you to do half."

The alternative, if I couldn't get the tension out of my jaw, would be surgery—"serious surgery," as Dr. Lassiter put it.

I went to see an acupuncturist religiously two or three times a week for six months and tried to relax more. I thought I was having success, but then the awful jolt of pain struck again with a vengeance. Dr. Lassiter recommended we proceed with the surgery.

By then we had learned more about tic douloureux symptoms, an ailment that mysteriously flourished in the late 1970s and 1980s. At the time there were only a handful of surgeons in the country qualified to do the surgery needed to repair the problem. Two of them were in Charlotte.

Mercy Hospital was the one place in town set up to do the kind of surgery I needed, so I went there. I wasn't worried. I knew when I went I was going to be okay. I wasn't the least bit anxious, but I had no idea the extent of the surgery I was about to undergo.

I woke up after the operation in the intensive care unit. Margie and Ron came to visit me shortly after I came to. I saw tears in their eyes.

"What's wrong?" I wanted to know.

"Nothing," they said. "You are all right. Everything is going to be all right."

A little later, Dr. Lassiter came in. "Sweetie Pie," he said, "you really gave us a shock."

"What? I did?" I was dumbfounded.

"No sooner had we opened up your skull," he explained to me, "then you had an aneurysm, one of the biggest I have ever seen. We had to remove part of your skull, but we caught it before it burst, or you wouldn't be with us here today."

I thought back to when I gave birth the first time, and thought, "Okay, Lord, that is strike two. You've saved me for a purpose twice now."

As it turned out, the expanding blood vessel is probably what was causing the tic douloureux symptoms, as the delicate nerve was being squeezed by the pressure.

I knew I had bandages wrapped all over my head and I was told to stay in bed and try to remain calm. The food was particularly awful, the worst I had ever had in a hospital, which didn't help. On my second day of recovery, I called for a nurse to help me relieve myself. When no one came, I called again; and when still nobody came, I oh-so-slowly slid out of bed, turning on my stomach to reach down with my feet and get them firmly planted on the floor. I started toward the bathroom, holding onto the edge of the bed. There was a sink across from the foot of the bed. Just as I reached out to grab the sink, I saw myself in the mirror for the first time following the surgery. I just started to scream! What I was seeing looked like something out of a horror movie. It was terrible. My face was black and blue and purple, and all swollen. I looked like a boxer who had been beaten to death.

Nurses came running when they heard me scream. I was crying, and they wanted to know what was wrong and why I was out of bed. That really was a low moment for me.

In the evening Dr. Lassiter came by and scolded me for getting out of bed. I begged him to let me go home, telling him how awful the food was. He apologized for not warning me about what I looked like, saying it looks a lot worse than it was. However, he did agree to let me go home, provided I would be good and not do anything more than rest and take it easy. He was rather stern about it.

"I'm going to tell you something," he said in a measured tone of voice. "You had brain surgery. This wasn't skull surgery. True, I had to go through your skull to get to your brain. But I worked on your brain. And the reason I am talking to you this way is so you will understand every word I am saying. You go home and don't think about going back to work or doing anything for four to six months. Do you hear me?"

His words made an impact on me. "Yes sir," I answered.

For eight weeks I didn't drive. I did do some work at home, but I stayed away from the office. Family members were wonderfully helpful. Someone was always coming by to make sure I wasn't getting into things I wasn't supposed to be doing.

People at work kept asking about me and it got to where they wanted to welcome me back to normal life. I was still afraid to be seen, even though my face had improved considerably and my hair had started to grow back. So I wrapped myself up like a Muslim woman with a headscarf on and went to a little reception they planned for me. Anytime people asked me why I was all covered up I told them, "You really don't want to see." But I appreciated the welcome back to normalcy, though I'd learned much about reality going through the experience.

Experiences like that can totally revamp a person's outlook on life. We take so much for granted. Life goes along and we don't realize how vulnerable we are, how fragile life is. It's like we live on a thin crust of ice covering a deep lake. At any time, without warning, the ice can break and we can find ourselves in a panic, gasping for breath in the icy chill, baffled at what has befallen us. Yes, with determination and the help of others, we can often get back on our feet again. But most people don't realize how close the danger lurks. Others who have been through traumatic crises are left with a lingering anxiety, unable to feel secure again. Learning to understand that life can take these shocking, unexpected turns is important. Just knowing that crises can occur helps us to be able to respond when one hits. But a crisis can also teach us much about what really matters in life.

We had a similar experience about twelve years ago when Ron had a series of heart attacks. We were vacationing in Alaska, enjoying a beautiful train ride from Fairbanks to Anchorage, when we began realizing that the spells Ron was having, which would leave him feeling utterly exhausted, might have something to do with his heart. In an Anchorage hospital he was diagnosed as needing bypass surgery. We flew him home on a Medivac plane, an airplane equipped to handle emergency cases, and had the surgery done in Charlotte.

He had been healthy looking and as active as ever up until the eve of our trip. Then, almost without warning, he was facing the biggest health crisis of his life. Like my ailment, his was also brought on by stress. One of the doctors told me afterward it was the worse case of stress damage he had ever seen and that Ron was a walking miracle. He'd actually had three heart attacks, any one of which could have killed him. Yet he came through without any permanent damage to his heart.

Following my experience I was left to reflect that what often drives us, what we really think is important, really isn't. I thought more about the near death experience I had when my first baby was born. I was learning again how things we fight so hard for, often material things, really are not that important.

What is important? I don't think there is a single soul on the face of the earth who has been created and not been given a purpose. We don't understand what that purpose is because we don't listen to what it is God is saying to us.

In the early 1960s I sought counseling from a Moravian minister. I guess I was feeling unsure of myself and, like my mother used to do, I was always saying "I'm sorry" to him. The minister finally stood up and threw his hands across the desk between us, completely startling me and making me jump out of my seat.

"Quit saying you're sorry," he said. "You are not doing anything wrong. You are not feeling anything wrong."

After our sessions we used to leave his office and go to the little chapel on the side of the church building, the "Little Church on the Lane," as he would call it. He would pray, "Lord, show this child the real love she has and how to bring it forth, and guide her in that direction."

Those moments in prayer did me so much good.

I was even more impressed when attending church there one Sunday. The ministers came down the aisle to hand out communion. When I was handed the bread, I hesitated. I had been taught you have to be a member of a church to participate in communion.

I whispered to the minister, "I'm not Moravian."

He whispered back to me, "Are you a child of God?"

"Yes," I said.

"Do you believe in Jesus Christ?" he asked.

"Of course," I replied.

"Take the bread," he told me.

I cried. I was overwhelmed by the realization that one didn't have to be a member of any human organization to be a child of God. We are automatically members of God's family. It was the most beautiful thing I had ever heard and it made me realize anew that our primary purpose in life is to experience and share the love of God.

I pray people will remember me as someone who experienced and shared the love of God.

Ron and I in a portrait we had taken in 1999.

THE GREATEST GIFT

For at least 31 years
You have been here beside us,
Giving us strength and love
Giving the power to guide us.

And through all this time
Together we've come far.
But tonight we want to show you
How special you really are.

You're not only our grandparents
You're our examples and our friends,
So if a helping hand is needed
Then we know our hearts you'll mend.

As you know, Christmas is about giving
And having your family together.
But you've given us the greatest gift,
A love that will last forever.

Jason ~ Lee ~ Christina ~ Tony ~ Natalie
Lydia ~ Londyn ~ Erica ~ Nathan~Benjamin
John ~ Dylan ~ Raphael ~ Leonardo

Appendix

Biographical Synopsis of
Katherine Hodges Harper

President, Harper Corporation of America
(Retired July 2006)

Technical Association of the Pulp Paper Industry (tappi)

1. Executive Council Corrugated Division.........1990–1994
2. Chairman Corrugated Division International Conference
   (First female in association's 46 year history). 1994
3. Officer and Chairman, Printing Committee,
   Corrugated Division ....Three years
4. National TAPPI Finance Committee ....Three years
5. National TAPPI Human Resource
   Development Committee .... Two years

Politics

1. Finance Chair, Mecklenburg County
   for Governor Jim Hunt during his campaign for the
   U.S. Senate 1984
2. U. S. Senate Candidate (NC)....................................1986

Government

Appointed by Governor:
1. NC Banking Commission...............................1983–1985
2. NC Advisory Board for
   Workforce Development................................1990–1992
3. NC Small Business Council...........................1993–1997

Appointed by U.S. Secretary of Commerce:
1. U. S. Export Council of North Carolina........1995–2000

BUSINESS

1. Co-founder,
   Harper Corporation of America...............1971
2. President, Harper Corporation of America
   and Harper Companies International............1978–2006
3. Co-founder,
   Harper Companies International...............1977
4. Corporate Secretary/Treasurer
   Harper/Love Adhesives ....1978 – 1991
5. Board of Directors,
   Harper/Love Adhesive................................1978 – 1991
6. Board of Directors,
   The Employers Association ....1995 – 2000

COMMUNITY

1. A Child's Place Advisory Board ....1992 – 1995

FOUNDATION OF FLEXOGRAPHIC TECHNICAL ASSOCIATION (FFTA)

1. Member of FFTA....................................... 1980–present
2. Co-contributor of $100,000 to One Million in Two
   Campaign *(Now Education and Research Fund)*
3. Served as chairman FFTA Forum
   (First female in 40 years history)......................................1995
4. Served on Steering Committee for
   Development of Future Forums 1995–1996
5. Co-developer of FFTA Flexo In High School Program
   (Now includes Colleges throughout the United States) 1991
6. Co-initiator of Ron & Katherine Harper
   Scholarship Fund..2003

EDUCATIONAL ACTIVITIES

1. Served on Appalachian State University
   Flexo Advisory Board 1999–2002
2. ASU Foundation Board *(Flexo Advocate)* 2002–2004
3. Central Piedmont Community College
   Foundation Board (Flexo Advocate)...............2002–2005

Special Awards

1. TAPPI Corporate Recognition
   Corrugated Container Division...............................1995
2. Special Award from Governor for
   Work Force Development 1995
3. Ben Franklin Award..1996
4. Central Piedmont Community College (CPCC)
   named a section the "Harper National
   Flexographic Center" 1998
5. Business Woman of the Year Award,
   Charlotte Business Journal 1999
6. CPCC named its Southwest Campus as
   the "Harper Campus" 2003
7. American Red Cross named "The Katherine Harper
   Disaster Staging Area" 2006
9. Katherine Harper Teacher's Education Fund
   established with the Phoenix Challenge Foundation ...2006
8. Katherine Harper Hall at Appalachian State University
   named in her honor...2007